D1432837

# BLUE COATS: BLACK SKIN

# BLUE COATS: BLACK SKIN

*The Black Experience in the New York City Police Department Since 1891*

# James I. Alexander

*An Exposition-University Book*

*Exposition Press*     *Hicksville, New York*

*To all Black officers
who risked their lives
in the building and structuring
of a democratic society,
and to their families,
who endured with them
in their experiences*

# Contents

# *Foreword*

This volume succinctly outlines and summarizes the history of the Black police officer in the New York City Police Department from 1891 to 1977 inclusive.

The author, James Alexander, has divided this period into five generations of Black officers who have served the city. Having been appointed to the police department as a patrolman in December, 1942, I fall into the third generation group (1931-1950).

Working conditions for the Black police officer at that time were almost unbearable, and we, in the third generation, were informed that they were even worse before 1931 and during the 1930s. The Police Academy Class of 1942 brought into the department the largest single group of Blacks at any one time. Previously, Blacks entered the department in small groups of two or three; we came as a group of approximately twenty. This posed somewhat of a problem, since the assignment of Black police officers had been confined, almost exclusively, to three precincts throughout the city—the 28th and 32nd Precincts in Central Harlem and the 79th Precinct in Bedford-Stuyvesant. Of the roughly 140 Black police officers on the 19,000 man force, I estimate that 130 of them were assigned to the three commands. The appointment, at the same time, of our large group forced a breakthrough, and the first Black was assigned to the 30th Precinct at 152nd Street in Washington Heights, and one was assigned to the Bronx.

Blacks at that time were almost never assigned to special assignments, such as the Detective Division, Plainclothes, Radio Motor Patrol, and were completely excluded from elite special squads, e.g., Missing Persons, Burglary, Forgery, Safe Loft and Truck, Pickpocket, Emergency Service, and so on.

As Mr. Alexander indicates, Black superior officers were almost nonexistent; Black officers received the most undesirable assignments; disciplinary actions against Blacks and against whites were uneven at the expense of the Blacks; and racial slurs by white patrolmen and superior officers against Black officers and Black citizens were commonplace.

Why, then, did Blacks enter the police department? The answer is simple—for economic reasons. Using a personal example, I entered the agency as a June, 1942, graduate of the City College of New York. The total number of college graduates in the department was almost nil, and Black college graduates could be counted on one hand. One member of my Police Academy class had even completed dental school. In 1942, a Black with a bachelor's degree in sociology could, at best, command a salary of $2,000 per year. Police officers, after a six months probationary period, started at $2,000 and progressed to $3,000 per year after *five* years.

These, then, were the conditions in 1942. The men who preceeded us, and those in the third and fourth generations, lived and worked under the most adverse conditions. Yet, most of them survived and retired with honor. Some, despite many obstacles, attained promotions of high responsibility.

Today, we find the fifth generation faced with yet the same problems encountered by preceding generations of Black police officers in the New York City Police Department. Too few Blacks enter the department for whatever reasons. Some claim that discriminatory testing practices still prevail. Others point to the negative image of the police department in minority communities. Promotions to higher rank, assignment to elite squads, and recognition for work accomplished continue to be limited to a very few Blacks.

In a period when the president of the United States raises aloft the banner of human rights for all throughout the world, it is shocking and regrettable that his message has not been clearly heard in our own land, in New York City, and in its police department. The protection and preservation of human rights has been entrusted by our citizens to the criminal justice system, of which police agencies are an integral part. If police officers are to serve as role models for our young people, much must be done by our society to make certain that every person wearing that uniform also possesses equal opportunity, equal rights, and equal privileges, just as those he protects.

Mr. Alexander, in *Blue Coats: Black Skin,* has compiled probably the most comprehensive book in America outlining the historical and current role of Black police officers in a major U.S. city. Perhaps its publication will hasten the day when all of our trustees of human rights will, themselves, fully receive their personal human rights.

ROBERT J. MANGUM,
*Judge of the Court of Claims,*
State of New York (formerly
Patrolman, Sergeant, Lieutenant,
Deputy Police Commissioner,)
1942-1958).

# Preface

It is said that a police officer's lot is not a happy one. Few occupations require the knowledge, skill, authority, and responsibility of his. There are times when he must make a split-second decision, one which may have lasting significance. He may be forced to take action resulting in the possible termination of a suspect's life or even his own. More often than not, a police officer's actions are judged a day, month, or years later. Hence, a police officer bears an awesome responsibility.

Because all police officers are so burdened—it comes with the job—the question arises why all police officers are not treated with equal admiration, respect, and general courtesy. The answer is that two systems of behavior exist governing police department procedures.

This double standard prevailed for so many years that members of the New York City Police Department have embraced it as the norm. Hence, there is little or no effort made on the part of the hierarchy in the department to foster a change in the prejudicial attitudes of the white police officers toward Blacks, Hispanics, and women—be they civilians or members of the force.

While serving as an officer of the New York City Police Department, I have had the opportunity to work with officers of various backgrounds. As a result of chance meetings on numerous occasions, I developed friendships with many officers. Some of these were Black and Hispanic officers who lost their lives in the performance of duty, such as Horace Lord, Ivan Lorenzo, and Joseph Taylor, to name a few. Why is it that minority personnel are treated with prejudice when statistics show that they are more likely to be seriously wounded or killed in the line of duty than their white counterparts?

I sincerely hope that this book will provide a better understanding of the role that Black police officers play in our society. Further, I hope that *Blue Coats: Black Skin* will act in some catalytic way to change the unfair, unequal systems that presently exist in the New York City Police Department.

# Acknowledgments

This book could not have been completed without both the cooperation of several institutions and the aid and encouragement of many people. I am particularly indebted to Howard Sheffey for providing valuable information and insight into the New York Police Department.

In addition, I received early encouragement from various people, especially from parents, brothers, and sisters of both my wife's family (the Dowdys) and mine, and from my friends and fellow workers.

The critical expertise and advice of the following people had much to do with what is good in this book: Professor Charles N. Piltch, Professor Lloyd Sealy, and Dr. Arthur Niederhoffer—all of John Jay College of Criminal Justice.

Special acknowledgment is due to the following persons who assisted in publishing this book: Robert W. Alexander, Jr., Dr. Warren St. James, Solomon Blackshear, Wilbert Bishop, William Jackson, Alan Davis, and Joseph Newkirk.

Perhaps my greatest indebtedness, however, is to my wife, Bettye, who consistently offered suggestions and alternatives when I was stymied and bolstered my spirits when I was low.

# BLUE COATS: BLACK SKIN

# I

## A Historical Perspective

A police officer's perception of the criminal justice system is based upon a number of complex factors. From the time that he joins a police department until the time he retires from it, the officer is constantly involved with interpersonal relationships with his fellow police officers. Therefore, the impressions that a police officer has of his department will depend, to a great extent, upon the type of treatment accorded him by members of that department. It is for this reason that some of the operating policies and procedures of the police are of crucial importance.

The interpersonal relationships between police officers are crucial in role-learning and creating a sense of identity.[1] Hence, the on-the-job experiences of Black police officers have helped to shape the view they have of themselves and of society. In turn, the view that white-majority police departments[2] have of Black police officers and Blacks in general have also been molded through social interaction. A variety of norms and values are transmitted through individual and group interaction. Values such as "self-esteem" and "group-status" will be directly affected by the type and method of police interaction.[3]

Although culture is learned through the group, not all learning through others is cultural. Only learning which is transmitted from generation to generation as part of the social heritage is cultural. A great deal of learning in which the cultural factor is subordinate or absent takes place in relation to other persons. Group interaction is common to life in all cultures, in all ages. Everywhere there is leading, following, teaching, imitating, intimidating, fighting, ostracizing, praising, blaming. These are general patterns of conduct, or forms of social behavior.[4]

As the result of social interaction, there is substantial evidence

3

connecting the relationship existing between Black and white police officers and the achieved status and self-esteem of Black and white police officers. Certain situations can accurately portray the increase and decline of status among Black police officers. These situations involve areas of Black accomplishments and failures that Blacks as police officers experienced as members of the New York City Police Department. Their experiences were in the forms of assignments, transfers, promotions, awards, and terminations due to layoffs, injuries, and death.

The intent of this study is to examine, verify, and classify the experiences of Black police officers on a generational basis. The generational experiences of Black officers will vary. This is due to the differences in the economic, social, and political circumstances experienced by each generation. It is also due to the variations in behavior that are peculiar to each individual in society. An individual's behavior is based to a great extent upon all previous events in his life that have had significance for him.

The scope of this study is limited to the period from 1891 to 1977. During this period five generations of Black police officers served the city of New York. Because of the large span of time covered in this study, emphasis has been placed upon specific Black police officers and on Black and white fraternal organizations in the New York City Police Department. Those areas of the Black police experience that are representative of their struggles, as well as their relationships with white police officers, are also depicted. In order to facilitate the classification and verification of the most important events involving Black officers, it was necessary to develop a historical chronology.

The New York City Police Department has been utilized in this study as a model of how a police department personnel's relationships affect the individual police officer and the department as a whole. It is felt that through the examination of the experiences among generations of Black New York City police officers, one will also gain a better understanding of the experiences that Black police officers shared while employed in other police departments.

The material presented in this study is basically divided into three areas: (1) a history of Blacks in the New York City Police Department, (2) interviews with active and retired Black and white police officers, and (3) biographical illustrations of the accomplishments and failures of important Black police officers.

Since it was important to develop a historical chronology, an extensive survey of the literature on Blacks was made. The following paragraphs represent some of the information that has been acquired through the selected works of specific authors.

The now defunct *Brooklyn Daily Eagle* newspaper assisted substantially in the identification and verification of the earliest Black police officers who served the cities of Greater New York. Particular credit is due Floyd G. Snelson for his pioneering work on pioneer Black policemen and Black firemen of New York City.[5] He also dealt with the presence of Black policemen in other cities throughout the United States. In more comprehensive surveys, the *Negro Yearbook* provided vital statistics on the number of Black policemen and policewomen in the United States during the years of 1916 through 1918. Similarly, Frank Mather, in his *Who's Who in the Colored Race,* supplied biographical information on certain Black police officers.[6]

Since an understanding of the interpersonal relationships between Black and white police officers was essential to this study, other works have been useful for background. Dr. Arthur Niederhoffer, in his *Behind the Shield,* examined the emotional and psychological facets of New York City police officers. He developed the concept of police secrecy, showing the effects that peer group pressure had upon police officers who broke the norms of the group. This was most important in understanding one of the causes for the rift between Black and white Police officers.[7]

In *Black in Blue,* Nicholas Alex examined and explained the variations in behavior among Black and white police officers. He underscored the ideological changes that younger Black police officers had undergone. He explained how these changes affected older Black officers, white officers, and the communities in which they served. In addition, he drew a relationship between the political changes in Black communities and how these changes affected the predominantly white police departments.[8]

Oscar Handlin in *The Newcomers* penetratingly examined New York City's minority group and their social, economic, and educational problems.[9] In *Race and Nationality in American Life,* Handlin presented an account of the rise and vicissitudes of two of the major concepts that dominate American life: race and nationality. He additionally demonstrated how these factors affected the fates of millions of Americans.[10]

In *Dark Ghetto,* Dr. Kenneth B. Clark explored possible solutions to the crime problems in the ghetto. Clark developed and elaborated upon the general Black perception of Black and white police officers. He also examined the view that Blacks in ghettos have of Black and white police officers. He demonstrated why Blacks viewed the police as repressive tools of the American system.[11]

In addition to the authors listed above, there were other sources that proved invaluable to this study. Newspapers such as the *New York Times, New York Amsterdam News,* and others provided an excellent source of information. Magazines like *Ebony* and *Jet* were also important contributors in this study.

However, it was found that there exists a scarcity of available information on Black police officers in the United States. In general, this reflects the lack of material on Blacks that exists in many other areas. Furthermore, there exists relatively little material on police officers from a historical point of view and throughout the country. Hence, it is not surprising to find a similar condition regarding the historical detailing of the New York City Police Department.

Unfortunately, for many years the New York City Police Department, like other police agencies, systematically destroyed unwanted files, books, and records in general. Thus, source material, which was produced during the various epochs in the history of the New York City Police Department, has been lost for all time.[12]

The earliest generation of Black police officers, in historical sequence, will be presented in chapter two. These police officers served in the city of Brooklyn prior to the consolidation of the various cities into the city of New York.[13] The span of time that this chapter will cover extends from 1891 through 1910. However, there exists a notable exception to this period of time, because of the inclusion of material relating to the year 1865.

In addition, this chapter exhibits the problems that Blacks in New York City, as well as other cities, faced before and after their appointments to the police force. It examines the age-old saying referring to Blacks as individuals and as a group in the employment market as "the last to be hired and the first to be fired."[14] There is also material that is descriptive of the general attitudes that Blacks as a group have shared in relationship to the police.

Innovation and change are clearly the underlying themes that are developed in chapter three. From 1911 to 1930, unparalleled "firsts" were achieved by a number of Black officers. The "firsts" were provided by men and women while in the service of their city and country. The "firsts" involved not only assignments to special police units but, moreover, promotions to rank within the New York City Police Department.

Chapter four will cover the third generation of Black police officers. In terms of time, this chapter will span the years from 1931 to 1950. It is during this period of time that the American public, as well as the world, experienced economic depression and war. While all of this was transpiring, Black New York City police officers were continuing their advancements to higher and still higher positions within the department. They strove to realize their aspirations and dreams not only as individuals but as a group. As a consequence, Black officers achieved mid-level and upper-level ranks in the city police department.

The fifth chapter will cover the fourth generation of Black New York City police officers from 1951 to 1970. Americans living during this period of time witnessed social, economic, and political upheaval not only in this country but in the world. These changes had tremendous ramifications upon the Black police officer. Some of the direct results would be manifested in the way certain Black officers within the New York City Police Department would be advanced to higher ranks. Hence, it is during this period that the term "spinoff-effect" would exist for those Black police officers that made rank (promotion) in the sixties while employed by the police department. This would be shown by their appointments to positions outside of the police department but nonetheless within the confines of the criminal justice system.

The sixth chapter covers the period of the early 1970s, from 1971 to 1977. It was during this period that the fifth generation of Blacks entered the department. The economic recession and the fiscal hardships that plagued the nation and the city of New York are shown to be some of the important factors that disproportionately affected Black, Hispanic, and female police officers. This chapter also deals with the problems that Black police officers faced while on duty as well as off duty. Finally, this chapter deals with the circumstances that led up to the dramatic split between the Guardians Association, a Black police fraternal association, and the Patrolmen's Benevolent Association (P.B.A.), the largest union in the New York City Police Department.

There will exist a type of generational overlapping in each chapter. The reason for this is basically a simple one: some of the achievements of one generation of Black police officers would reach prominence in the early years of the succeeding generation of Black officers. The importance of this condition is clearly established throughout the chapters. The acquired status of each generation of Black officers is due in part to the cumulative effect that the preceding generation of officers has upon the one that succeeds it.

## NOTES

1. John J. Honigmann, *Personality in Culture* (New York: Harper and Row Co., 1967), p. 175.
2. Abraham S. Blumberg, *Criminal Justice* (New York: Quadrangle Books, 1970), p. xxviii.
3. Melvin M. Tumin, *Social Stratification* (Englewood Cliffs, N.J.: Prentice Hall, 1967), pp. 35-37, 52, 54-55.

4. William F. Ogburn and Meyer F. Nimkoff, *Sociology* (Boston: Houghton Mifflin, 1968), p. 211.

5. Floyd Snelson, "Negro Policemen and Firemen," 27 July 1927 to 6 February 1930, Federal Writers Project (microfilm), Schomberg Collection, Reel 3, Article 28, n.p.

6. Frank Lincoln Mather, ed. *Who's Who of the Colored Race* (Chicago: Memento Edition, 1915), passim.

7. Arthur Niederhoffer, *Behind the Shield: The Police in Urban Society* (New York: Doubleday & Co., 1967), passim.

8. Nicholas Alex, *Black in Blue* (New York: Appleton-Century Crofts, 1969), passim.

9. Oscar Handlin, *The Newcomers* (New York: Doubleday & Company, 1962), passim.

10. Oscar Handlin, *Race and Nationality in American Life* (New York: Doubleday and Co., 1950), passim.

11. Kenneth B. Clark, *Dark Ghetto* (New York: Harper & Row, 1965), passim.

12. Interview with Detective Al Young, historian for the New York City Police Department, May, 1975.

13. Gerald Astor, *The New York Cops* (New York: Charles Scribner's Sons, 1971), passim.

14. Herbert Blumer, "Race Prejudice as a Sense of Group Position," in Jitsuichi Masuoka and Preston Valien, eds., *Race Relations* (Chapel Hill, N.C.: The University of North Carolina Press, 1961), pp. 215-27.

# II

## *Black Pioneers*

During the period of 1891 to 1910, the first generation of Blacks entered the New York City Police Department. Although there is evidence relating to one Black police officer on the city of New York's Police Department in 1865, Blacks as a group entered the department in the 1890s. This period of time would prove extremely important for Blacks, especially for Black men and women who would later join the police department.

What we know about the experiences of the first generation of Black police officers may appear, at first glance, to be miniscule; however, the Blacks that entered the police force during this period did so under tremendous social, economic, and political stress. Hence, even to be appointed to the police department was an accomplishment. To serve the department and the community without receiving disciplinary action was also an accomplishment. However, the most impressive accomplishment was that more than one Black police officer managed to *survive* long enough to retire from the department and, additionally, to collect a pension.[1]

This period of history is also representative of the phrase "getting one's foot in the door." This particular concept applied to Blacks involved in attempting to secure employment for themselves and their families.[2] Similarly, Blacks literally would begin to "get their feet in the doors" of the police department in the city of New York—Blacks would at first be assigned to police precincts as doormen but, would eventually, through the years rise to the highest ranks in the police department.[3]

The occupational experiences that were shared by the first generation of Blacks on the police force would also be shared, on a similar basis, by succeeding generations of Black police

11

officers. In part, this was due to the early establishment of behavioral and attitudinal responses on the part of the white membership of the force toward the Black membership. Thus,
unfortunately, a pattern of discrimination and bias toward Blacks
would develop and persist through the years in the department.
In many respects this condition still exists today. The rationale
behind it will be established in part by the material that is to
follow.

The pattern of mistreatment that has been accorded to Blacks
in this country has often been referred to as "Jim Crow." The
use of this term became commonplace during the nineteenth
century and referred to any law, any ordinance, and any custom
that kept Blacks apart from whites and prevented them from
freely participating in the mainstream of American life. This
policy was particularly manifest following the Civil War in
the United States. It was during the post-Civil War era that whites
regained control of the southern legislatures. Afterward, they
began to pass Jim Crow laws. These laws, in many cases, put an
end to the gains that Blacks had achieved earlier while they
were playing a more active role in the social, economic, and
political life of the South.[4]

Much of today's Black population found in the northern
urban centers of this country is a basic result of the early migration of Blacks from the South during the post-Civil War era.
Because of the economic conditions of the South, many Black
families were held in virtual slavery while working to pay debts
that mounted viciously and, in many cases, without end. Many
of these debts were passed from one generation to the next.
Against this system Black men and women labored to acquire
land, to educate their children, and to find a way to live as decent
human beings. Many Black families began to despair and to feel
that there was no hope for them in the South. As a result numerous Black families began to pack their belongings, scrape together
what little money they had, and leave the South.[5]

The first movement of the "Great Exodus" began in 1879,
and although it was the largest and most dramatic outflow of
Blacks from the South, it established a trend and a pattern that

still continues. Many of these Black families left the South for the industrial cities of the North. These families took with them hopes of finding living conditions, at least, somewhat better than those of the South.[6]

As a direct result of the Black migration, the cities of Greater New York experienced a sudden and dramatic increase in its Black population. Two of the cities that experienced the highest influx of Blacks were Brooklyn (Kings County) and New York (Manhattan County).[7] As a result of the migration of Blacks into northern cities, certain groups exerted political pressure upon Congress to do something about it. Some Congressional leaders were able to set up a commission that was empowered to investigate the matter and to report back to their constituency. However, nothing of legal consequence could be brought to bear upon the Blacks leaving the South.[8]

As people began to become concerned about the movement of Blacks from one place of the country to another, Black men became the open target for a growing wave of violence. In the decade between 1890 to 1899, an average of two Black men per week were lynched in the United States. From 1882 to 1938, the number of Blacks lynched in the United States totalled 3,397. Some of these lynchings occurred outside the southern states. In fact, some of the first Black police officers worked in the same areas where Blacks had experienced overt hostility. Hence, the early Black police officer worked under adverse conditions.[9]

Not only did Blacks living during this period have to endure economic hardships and terrorism, there existed, additionally, a rise in the racist-thinking among the native inhabitants of northern cities. Coupled to this dilemma were elaborate forms of social discrimination. One of these forms involved compulsory segregation of the races in public establishments and facilities. This condition was further reinforced when the Supreme Court of the United States ruled in 1896, in the case of *Plessy* v. *Ferguson,* that the state segregation laws did not violate the Fourteenth Amendment of the Constitution as long as the separate facilities, one for Blacks and the other for whites, were in fact equal. Thus, the federal government's abandonment of Blacks was substantially proved, for the "separate but equal doctrine" thereafter gave the South, and some northern areas of the country, the green light to impose massive legal regulations regarding segregation. Hence, Blacks by law were treated to the "white racial superiority" concept. But in reality, no one really bothered to insure that the separate facilities for Blacks were in fact equal to those of whites.[10]

Lacking a sound social, economic, and political framework for his own self-defense, the Black man found himself at the mercy of the whims of white lawmakers and law enforcers. With such circumstances in mind, one can readily understand why, during this period from 1865 through 1910, there existed the natural tendency of many Blacks to lapse into an attitude of acquiescence bordering on servility. One philosopher who seemed to fit the mood of these times was Booker T. Washington. Although a former slave, Washington emerged in the late nineteenth and early twentieth centuries as a leading spokesman for Black aspirations. He suggested in his numerous lectures and speeches that for the time being Blacks should put aside their aspirations for full political and social equality and concentrate on developing vocational training and acquiring work skills. He felt that this would enable Blacks to improve their economic position. He further lectured on the notion that Blacks might eventually and gradually convince whites of their genuine worth as productive citizens. Thereafter, the white majority might be willing to accord Blacks the social, economic, and political rights that were due them.[11]

The foregoing type of attitude regarding "race relations" was generally accepted by Blacks and generally greeted by whites.[12] As a result of this type of thinking, Blacks did not feel that it was in their best interest to pursue efforts in areas in which Blacks were few in number, let alone, pursue employment in fields that had traditionally excluded Blacks. This applied to the field of law enforcement as well as many other fields. Since Blacks had received unequal treatment by the law and by law enforcers, it was hardly a common practice on the part of Blacks to seek employment in a police department. Hence, a Black man applying for the position of patrolman during this period of history was "going against the system." The first Black applicants for the position of patrolman[13] or doorman[14] had to be of staunch character. Any Black applicant could expect a hard time of it from not only the whites in the law enforcement agency, but also Blacks who had become suspicious of policemen over the years. However, Blacks did begin to join the police departments in the northern cities. Many of these first Black police officers' heritage was based upon a southern background, for many of them had personally migrated to a particular northern city or had been incorporated into a Black family's migration from the South. As a matter of fact, many of the northern Black police officers now have a basic southern background. This life experience was also shared by the first Black policemen in the city of Greater New York.[15]

The first Black policeman to serve the city of New York has long been regarded, officially, as Samuel Jesse Battle.[16] Although it would be accurate to state that Battle was the first Black appointed to the New York City Police Department after the consolidation of the cities in 1898, he was not in fact the first Black New York City police officer to serve in the department. This is based upon a very important and technical reason, in that the various boroughs that are presently incorporated in the city of New York were individual cities before 1898. Hence, police services prior to 1898 were under separate city jurisdictions, because the cities of Brooklyn, New York, Richmond, Bronx, and Queens had their own municipal governments and agencies. However, after the consolidation of these cities into one city, New York City, many of the employees who worked under separate municipal agencies continued their employment under agencies within New York City. In a similar way, many police officers serving various cities were incorporated into the New York City Police Department. Since there were Black police officers in the Brooklyn Police Department prior to the consolidation of the cities, some of these Black police officers continued their employment, but as policemen in the city of New York. For more than a decade, there were Black police officers on the force before Samuel Jesse Battle's appointment to the force in 1911.[17]

The earliest evidence of a Black police officer in the cities of Greater New York is contained in a photograph dated 1865. Represented in the photograph are four police officers assigned to the 32nd precinct. It was taken on the corner of 152nd Street and 10th Avenue. Unfortunately, the exact identity of the Black policeman in the photograph is presently unattainable. However, by examining the photograph, the viewer would see the following: (a) all of the officers, including the Black officer, are attired in the uniform of the day; (b) the Black officer, along with the other white officers, is holding the reins to a horse. This leads one to believe that all four of these officers, apart from the others in the photograph, were probably part of the "Old Mounted Squadron" attached to the 32nd Precinct.[18]

Thus, there was a Black police officer in the city of New York in 1865. Bear in mind, that the Civil War had just ended and that there were Blacks who participated in it, some fighting on the side of the North as foot-soldiers and as cavalrymen. I suppose it would be speculative to assume that the Black officer in the photograph served in the Union forces; however, there exists substantial evidence to support the fact that Blacks did fight on both sides in the Civil War.[19] There also exists evidence to support the notion that the officer may have had prior military experience, for many of the returning Black soldiers entered various municipal agencies prior to Jim Crow restrictions on employment.[20]

It is not until twenty years later that there exists documented evidence indicating the presence of another Black officer in the cities of Greater New York. This came about in March of 1891 when Wiley G. Overton was appointed to Brooklyn's department. Police Commissioner Hayden, of the Brooklyn Police Department, appointed Overton to the position of patrolman and assigned Overton to the 1st Precinct, which was commanded by Captain Campbell. Overton's first assignment was to a footpost on Hudson Avenue and Navy Street. Thus, Wiley G. Overton may have become the first Black appointed to the city of Brooklyn's police force and the first Black police officer to walk a beat in the city of Brooklyn.[21]

On July 17, 1891, Captain Campbell was interviewed by a newspaper reporter for the *Brooklyn Daily Eagle*. When questioned regarding Overton, Captain Campbell responded with the following remarks:

> Yes, I have decided to place Overton on special duty in the colored district of which Hudson Avenue is a central point. There is nothing at all surprising in that, is there? If I had an Italian policeman, wouldn't I naturally assign him to duty in the Italian quarter. As a matter of fact, the captain of the 4th Precinct and myself have had a good deal of trouble in the colored district lately and have been compelled to keep men there. I propose to try the experiment of having my colored officer down there for a while and I will probably assign him there today. But the change is not permanent and Overton is, if able, to return to general work at any time. I have other policemen on special details in parts of the precinct.[22]

The interviewing reporter concluded that Overton was better fitted for duty in special quarters than for general routine police work. The rationale for this reporter's opinion was that Overton had labored under a decided disadvantage since he became a member of the force. The men at the Adam Street station had steadily ignored him. There was also an indication of mutiny as a result of the appointment of Overton to the department and his assignment to the 1st Precinct. This situation was smothered by the firmness of Commissioner Hayden and Captain Campbell. As a result of their actions, the officers assigned to the 1st Precinct made up their minds to quietly ignore Overton. Hence, Overton's position in the department was anything but enviable. He was left severely alone by his "associates" who refused to talk with him unless it was absolutely necessary, that is, in the line of duty. Overton was as much alone in the stationhouse as if he were on a desert island, as far as indications of friendliness went. The reporter went on to conclude that Overton had been stunted by the behavior on the part of the other police officers. The result was that Overton never received the benefits of the kindly hints and assistance given by the men to recruits in their ranks. Therefore, Overton had to feel his way alone. The result was that many little points of police work had not been acquired by him. In addition to the foregoing reasons, the consensus of opinion shared by the membership of the Brooklyn Police Department was in favor of Overton's being assigned to the Black quarter of the city.[23]

As a result of the hostility shown toward him by the white membership of the police force, Overton suffered psychological and emotional trauma. The white police officers' behavior told Overton that a Black man was not wanted in the police department. This attitude had a detrimental effect upon Overton's identity as a man in society who happened by birth to be Black. Since people provide us with new aspirations of what we should like to be and of what we should like to appear to be, Overton's aspirations were not reinforced but in fact undermined and possibly utterly destroyed. Also since people provide us with models of conduct from which we draw confirmation of our own identity, Overton was not provided an acceptable occupational model from which he could draw the essential knowledge needed to develop his own talents as a police officer. Overton's own incentive to continue on in his field was not the least bit encouraged by the Brooklyn Police Department.[24]

On Wednesday, December 28, 1892, Overton made a written proposal to Commissioner Hayden asking permission to resign from the force on or about January 1, 1893. Overton also wanted to be placed on "day duty" during the month in order that he might have a chance of attending night school as preparation for the civil service position of clerk in the federal government.[25]

Overton served the city of Brooklyn and its police department for one year and eight months before resigning on January 11, 1893. He was still seeking a clerk's position with the federal government at the time of his resignation. As a matter of fact,

Overton enlisted the aid of two Congressmen, Wagner and Clancy.[26]

While Wiley G. Overton was a member of the Brooklyn Police Department, three other Black police officers also served there. However, the brunt of the hostility by whites was directed toward Overton, based upon events that unfolded during his tenure as a police officer. For on Monday, April 25, 1892, members of the police department in the city of Brooklyn were disturbed over the fact that there were three Black men among those (whites) on the eligibility list for the position of patrolman. The opinion of the white police officers and white political groups was that unless the police commissioner assigned the three Black officers to duty, after their appointment to the force, as doormen, there would surely be trouble. The undercurrent of disfavor may have suggested another episode of a mutiny on the part of the Brooklyn police force.[27]

However, the police commissioner could not avoid the appointment of the three Black men to the force, for they had passed the civil service examination and were high on the list of eligible candidates for the position of police officer. In addition, it was also known that a prominent Black attorney, T. McCants Stewart, had already stated that he would take the case of the three Black men to court if Commissioner Hayden failed to appoint them to the force.[28] The three men in question were Moses P. Cobb of 437 Hudson Avenue, Philip W. Hadley of 449 Adelphi Street, and John W. Lee of 487 Myrtle Avenue. All of these Black men lived in the Black district in the City of Brooklyn.[29]

Following the example set by Patrolman Overton, Cobb, Hadley, and Lee had themselves examined by three separate and "first-class' physicians in the city of New York prior to being examined by the city of Brooklyn's police surgeon. If the men were rejected by the police surgeon, they would apply to the courts for redress. The behavior exhibited by these men, Overton, Cobb, Hadley, and Lee, obviously underscored their genuine mistrust of the police department's fairness and equitability regarding its dealings with Blacks in general.[30]

On Saturday, May 14, 1892, Moses P. Cobb, along with

eighteen other men, was appointed to the Brooklyn Police Department. Afterward, Cobb was assigned to the 12th Precinct.[31] Cobb's being assigned to this specific precinct was based upon the similar concept regarding the assignment of Overton to the 1st Precinct; both precincts contained a large Black population and the police department hoped that their being assigned to these areas would ease the tension between the Black community and the members of the police department. Although the commanding officer of the 12th Precinct, Captain Dryer, felt that Cobb would be useful at that precinct, he nonetheless indicated a concern for the reception that the Black officer would receive at the Atlantic Avenue station house.[32]

Although Moses P. Cobb began his career in the Brooklyn Police Department as a "doorman," his assignment was eventually changed and he worked as a footpatrolman with general duties. Police Officer Cobb also continued to serve as a policeman after the consolidation of the cities into one in 1898. Thus, Moses P. Cobb was on the New York City Police Department before and after the appointment of Samuel Jesse Battle to the force in 1911.[33]

After serving the public and the department for twenty-five years, Police Officer Cobb retired from the force in 1917.[34] He was one of the longest serving Black policemen in the history of the department during this period.[35]

In August of 1892, Philip W. Hadley became the third Black man appointed to the Brooklyn police force. He was assigned as a "doorman" as a result of political pressure exerted by certain political factions that opposed the assignment of Hadley to general police work.[36]

On Tuesday, November 29, 1892, Commissioner Hayden dealt with forty-two men charged with violating the rules and procedures of the department. Some of these men were charged with sleeping while on duty and with being intoxicated while on duty. Patrolman Hadley was the first officer out of the forty-two policemen to see the police commissioner. He was charged with being intoxicated and unfit for duty. Upon seeing Officer Hadley, Hayden immediately dismissed Hadley from the force. All of the other policemen, many of whom had been charged with more serious violations of the rules and procedures, were merely fined and docked vacation days and days off. None of the forty-one white police officers lost his job as a result of his appearance before the police commissioner.[37] Hence, there existed a double standard in the Brooklyn Police Department, one for its Black members and one for its white members, separate and unequal. Philip W. Hadley served the city of Brooklyn for only four short months before being dismissed from the force.

On December 8, 1892, John W. Lee was sworn in by Commissioner Hayden as a police officer in the Brooklyn Police Department. Thus, Lee became the fourth Black police officer to be appointed to Brooklyn's police department. After Lee's appointment to the force, he was assigned to the 21st Precinct as a "doorman."[38] Patrolman Lee continued to serve as a police officer after the consolidation of the cities in 1898.[39] He served as a footpatrolman while under the jurisdiction of the New York City Police Department. In addition, Patrolman Lee was also on the force prior to and after the appointment of Samuel Jesse Battle to the New York City Police Department in 1911.[40]

On August 19, 1924, John W. Lee retired from the new York City Police Department, thereby becoming the longest serving Black police officer in the history of the department, for he had served thirty-two years on the force. He was assigned to the Clinton Avenue Precinct at the time of his retirement.[41]

Sometime in 1893, John W. Nelson was appointed to the Brooklyn Police Department. Nelson was assigned as a "doorman" to the Butler Street station house in Coney Island.[42] On Friday, December 14, 1900, Patrolman Nelson was arrested by Patrolman Kearns at a bar called Dolan's. Nelson was brought to the Adams Street station house and charged with being intoxicated and threatening to shoot the owner of the bar, Dolan. Nelson appeared before Judge Brennen and was suspended and then later dismissed from the police department.[43] John W. Nelson had served the Brooklyn police force for seven years before being dismissed from the department.[44]

In the autobiography of Thomas Roy Peyton, Jr., M.D.,

there exists evidence that there was another Black policeman on
the Brooklyn Police Department prior to the consolidation of
this city police force into the New York City Police Department.[45]
This police officer was the father of Dr. Peyton, Thomas Roy
Peyton, Sr. In the autobiography, Peyton, Jr. indicates that sometime in 1895 his father walked a beat in Brooklyn. His father
was assigned to the old Traffic "D" station house near the East
River.[46] Unfortunately, no other information concerning Thomas
Roy Peyton, Sr., could be obtained.

In 1897, the charter for the creation of Greater New York
passed the state legislature. In 1898, the city of Brooklyn lost
its separate identity and New York City was expanded to take
in the five boroughs (cities) that it presently includes in its
jurisdiction. All police forces within the enlarged city limits were
now consolidated into the New York City Police Department.
The governing body of this force remained a four-man board of
commissioners, divided equally between the major political parties
of this period and appointed by the mayor of New York City.
The chief of police had the power to assign and transfer policemen and to suspend erring members for up to ten days, pending
trial by one or more of the commissioners. Promotions were to
be made by the board but applicants had to have a written
recommendation by the chief, unless the office of the chief was
vacant. Each of New York City's boroughs had a deputy chief. A
unanimous vote of the board, or a majority of the board coupled
with the consent of the mayor, had the power to retire the chief
or any of the deputy chiefs. Police department appointments
were made under the regular civil service machinery, which
operated for the benefit of the political party that was in power.[47]

In 1901, the police board was abolished and a police commissioner was appointed by the mayor of New York City. The first
commissioner of the New York City Police Department was
Michael C. Murphy.[48]

In the nineteenth century, New York was not a well-policed
city. Although the force did grow considerably during the 1890s,
especially after the consolidation of the cities, the police department by no means achieved professional status.[49] George Walling,

who had forty years of police service, noted that many of the stereotypes caused by poor police-community relationships were reinforced by the behavior of the membership of the police department. He saw the public as being demoralized to such an extent that they no longer considered the policeman in his true light. They actually, with some degree of justice, saw the policeman as an enemy. However, Walling also understood another concept of human behavior, for he was aware that the negative attitude on the part of the community would react upon the policeman until he (the policeman) would very naturally consider himself not unlike an armed soldier in the midst of a hostile camp.[50]

The alienation of the police force from the community was further increased by the social, economic, and political problems involving Blacks and whites. This was manifested by the riot of August 15, 1900, and by the subsequent whitewashing of the entire matter. The riot grew out of the competition for jobs and living accommodations between the Irish and Blacks. This situation had become a focal point for many of the political leaders of this period. The problems involving Blacks and whites were found, more often than not, in the cities of Brooklyn and New York. While the Black population increased in the Hudson Street area of Brooklyn, in a similar way the Black population increased along the West Thirties in New York. After the classical precipitating incident of a fatal fight between a Black civilian and a white policeman, rampaging crowds moved up and down 8th and 9th avenues beating Blacks. Policemen swarmed over the area, cracking the heads of Blacks, while doing nothing to restrain the Irish mob. Frank Moss, a political activist of this period, carefully gathered testimony concerning the police brutality and pressured the police commissioner to take some proper disciplinary action against those police officers who were involved in the melee. The police commissioner did agree with Frank Moss to set up department hearings; however, in every case the commissioner refused to allow counsel for the Black plaintiffs to cross-examine witnesses favoring the police, and whenever there was conflicting testimony the police commissioner would accept the word of the policeman involved. The police commissioner explained to the mayor of New York City that when a police witness testified he did so in an impartial manner, while the witnesses for the plaintiffs "displayed a strong and bitter feeling while under examination." The entire proceedings were a miscarriage of justice. If Blacks exhibited some bitterness while under questioning it is hardly surprising, since the police did not protect them from the Irish mob but did in fact join the mob and indulge in the gratuitous clubbing of Blacks.[51]

The period of 1891 to 1910 was one of failure, disgust, and disappointment for many Blacks in the city of New York. Likewise, many of the Blacks appointed to the Brooklyn Police Department experienced similar feelings. Although there was possibly only a handful of Black policemen who survived long enough to become a part of the New York City Police Department and to be able to collect a police pension, their accomplishments represent an important epoch for Blacks as a group and as individuals. Police officers like Cobb and Lee set an example of endurance and steadfastness that other succeeding generations of Black policemen would have to follow if they too would accomplish their particular goals.

It can be accurately stated that the first generation of Black New York City police officers were true "pioneers." These first Black officers had secured employment, no matter how short or long, in a field that was formally occupied only by whites. They had experienced police work, no matter how trivial or routine, which was important historically, for it was a beginning for Blacks in law enforcement in the city of New York.

## NOTES

1.  James F. Richardson, *The New York Police* (New York: Oxford University Press, 1970), p. 174. Police officers had to serve a minimum of twenty years in order to be eligible for retirement benefits.
2.  Handlin, *Race and Nationality in American Life,* pp. 136, 137.

3. *Brooklyn Daily Eagle,* 1890.

4. Roy Stannard Baker, *Following the Color Line* (New York: Harper & Row Publishers, 1964), p. 30.

5. Bradford Chambers, *Chronicles of Black Protest* (New York: New American Library, 1968), p. 134.

6. Ibid., p. 135.

7. Handlin, *The Newcomers,* p. 47.

8. Langston Hughes, Eric Lincoln, Milton Meltzer, *The Pictorial History of Black Americans* (New York: Crown Publishers, 1975), p. 219.

9. Chambers, p. 139.

10. Joseph J. Huthmacher, *A Nation of Newcomers* (New York: Dell Publishing Co., Inc., 1967), pp. 80-81.

11. Baker, pp. 219-23.

12. Earl E. Thorpe, *Black Historians* (New York: William Morrow and Co., Inc., 1971), pp. 61-65.

13. Patrolman-Police Officer—Authority to carry a gun, power of arrest, patrol, investigate, and all other general duties performed and required of a patrolman.

14. Doorman—Responsible for securing the front door of the Police Station House, opening the door for police personnel and guests, and custodial duties.

15. All of the first Black police officers in the city of Brooklyn were born in the South.

16. *New York Times,* 28 June 1911.

17. Police officers Moses P. Cobb and John W. Lee served both the cities of New York and Brooklyn, before and after the consolidation.

18. Courtesy of Alfred J. Young (Alfred J. Young Collection), New York City Police Department's historian.

19. Thorpe, pp. 172-80.

20. Ibid., pp. 192-93.

21. *Brooklyn Daily Eagle,* March 1891.

22. Ibid., 17 July 1891.

23. Ibid.

24. Edward C. McDonagh and Jon E. Simpson, *Social Problems: Persistent Challenges* (New York: Holt, Rinehart & Winston, Inc., 1965), pp. 88-95.

25. *Brooklyn Daily Eagle,* 28 December 1891.
26. Ibid.
27. *Brooklyn Daily Eagle,* 25 April 1892.
28. Ibid.
29. Ibid.
30. Many of the prospective Black candidates for civil service positions would be knocked off the appointment lists due to "alleged" physical defects. One of the most common was the "heart murmur."
31. *Brooklyn Daily Eagle,* 14 May 1892.
32. Ibid.
33. Officer Moses P. Cobb served for nineteen years before the appointment of Samuel Jesse Battle to the police department of the City of New York.
34. *Amsterdam News,* 7 May 1966.
35. Police Officer Moses P. Cobb served from May 14, 1892, until 1917. Thus, he served twenty-five years, second only to Officer John W. Lee.
36. *Brooklyn Daily Eagle,* August 1892.
37. Ibid., 29 November 1892.
38. Ibid., 8 December 1892.
39. Spring 3100, "Police Facts," Bulletin No. 18 (1973): 4.
40. Police officer John W. Lee served nineteen years before Samuel Jesse Battle was appointed to the force.
41. *New York Times,* 19 August 1924.
42. *Brooklyn Daily Eagle,* 14 December 1900.
43. Ibid.
44. Ibid.
45. Thomas Roy Peyton, Jr., *A Quest for Dignity, Autobiography of a Negro Doctor* (Los Angeles: Warren F. Lewis, 1950), pp. 5-7.
46. Ibid., p. 7.
47. Richardson, pp. 268-69.
48. Spring 3100, p. 10.
49. Richardson, p. 284.
50. Ibid., p. 191.
51. Ibid., p. 276.

# III

## *The Breakthrough Years*

From 1911 to 1930, the second generation of Black police officers entered the New York City Police Department. It would be during this period that Black officers would achieve "firsts" in the department. These firsts would materialize in the form of appointments, assignments, and promotions of Black officers. One of these would be the appointment of the first Black police officer to the New York City Police Department after the consolidation of the cities into that of Greater New York. Another would be the appointment to the force of the first Black policewoman. Still others would be the promotion to the rank of sergeant and the ranking status of detective for Black officers. Although there would be numerous firsts by other generations of Black officers, the firsts achieved by the second generation of Black officers would represent the breakthroughs that were necessary for the generations of Black officers to follow.

The occupational experiences of the second generation of Black officers would form a pattern and develop a pace for succeeding generations of Black officers. Their experiences, occupational as well as "off duty," would be related to those experiences shared by Blacks in the nation. Within the context of economic, social, and political change, national and local events would affect both Black and white police officers. Therefore, this chapter should begin with the important historical events affecting Blacks in this period.

After 1910, Black people began to hope for a change in their lives. The National Association for the Advancement of Colored People (N.A.A.C.P.) and the National Urban League were just beginning their work when World War I broke out.[1] The war aroused in the Black population a new hope for restoration of

their rights and a new militancy in demanding first-class citizen-
ship. More than 360,000 of them entered military service and a
large part of those saw overseas duty in uniform.[2]

During World War I, Black officers in the armed forces led
men who won many honors in Europe. The 369th Regiment from
New York engaged the enemy in battle on numerous occasions
and their efforts won them many victories.[3]

While the war was on in Europe, Black people left the Jim
Crow world of the South and migrated to the cities of the North.[4]
By early 1919, thousands of Black soldiers had returned home to
the United States. Nearly 3,000 Black soldiers, alone, returned
to New York City.[5] After the Black troops returned to the States,
they, along with other Black people, began to hope and press for
an end to discrimination and segregation. However, the whole
country seemed to grow more conservative. The country (whites)
turned against change and people tried to maintain life as it had
been for generations. As a result, a wave of riots shocked the
country. In city after city, Blacks and whites fought in the
streets.[6]

During the early 1920s, the leaders of government, like most
white Americans, continued to oppose change. Hate groups
appeared on the scene. The Ku Klux Klan began to grow stronger
and flex its muscles in the form of brutality against Blacks. Anti-
Semitic activities grew. Anti-Catholic feeling spread. White hate
groups seemed to adopt the Klan thinking to the detriment of all
minority groups. As a result of the foregoing conditions, the
N.A.A.C.P.'s first national campaign began in the 1920s. On
behalf of Blacks, the N.A.A.C.P. waged a fight to secure federal
legislation against the beating and the lynching of Black citizens.
(This barbarous practice had cost hundreds of Blacks their lives
without the benefit of a court trial.) The decade of the 1920s was
an inauspicious period for the cause of minority rights and, by
its close, the N.A.A.C.P. and its allies had little to show for their
efforts.[7]

Although the gains in legislation and in case law were not
forthcoming from this country's leadership, there were substantial

changes in other areas of American life. For a large number of young people, both Black and white, were ready to turn against many of the old ideas. They looked for a new kind of freedom— freedom to do as they pleased. They drank a great deal even though a federal law had made it a crime to sell liquor. They danced a great deal. They turned to the kind of music called jazz. The automobile, new then, gave them even more freedom.

In the Black areas of large cities located in the northern states, the "Age of Jazz" was affecting the lives of millions of Americans. In Harlem, the Black population had grown enormously. During this period, Harlem became the "Blacks' (as well as national) Mecca" for Black culture. It was the "Harlem Renaissance."[8]

In October, 1929, the stock market crashed. In its wake began the longest and most severe depression in American history. At the height of the depression decade, there were 14,000,000 unemployed Black and white workers.[9]

By 1930, Black workers in the cities and on the farms had many problems. Most farmers in the South were tenant farmers. The owners of the land they farmed were beginning to buy more farm machinery. This meant fewer farmers were needed. Machines could do more work than any man. Black farmers and their families moved from the South to the North in a steady flow. Once in the cities they found that their farming skills did not mean much. They had to begin again. This meant the lowest-paying jobs, usually in the factories. It meant that they had to work as servants or take menial jobs in stores and restaurants. Low pay brought no real improvement in the way a Black family could live. To add to this economic instability, the old Jim Crow fear was still present. This was found in the way the Black worker was treated on the job. He would be the last hired and the first fired![10]

It is vitally important that the reader be aware that the salary of police officers in New York City was fairly high in comparison to the salaries of other types of occupations during this period of time. For example, the salary for first-grade patrolman was

$1400 in 1914. By the year 1921, the salary had risen to $2280, which is an increase of $880, or 61 percent over the salary for police officers in 1914.[11] In addition to the above salary benefits, the police officer's wife and family (immediate sons and daughters) received health and welfare benefits, and the city of New York provided for a retirement pension for police officers who completed the prescribed years of service to the city.

Hence, it was economically as well as socially advantageous for a family to have their father or husband employed as a New York City police officer. Thus, there can be little doubt as to the rationale behind Blacks' attempting to join the police force. This was manifested earlier in 1907 when African Methodist Episcopal (A.M.E.) Bishop Reverdy Ransome, of Harlem, organized a coalition of Black workers, political groups, church groups, and neighborhood groups for the purpose of securing the position of police officer for qualified Black men. For since the consolidation of the cities of Brooklyn, Queens, Richmond, Manhattan, and the Bronx into one city, there had not been any Blacks appointed to the city's police department.

During the spring of 1907, Bishop Ransome led a large coalition of Black and white citizens from Harlem, as well as from other parts of the city, in a rally at City Hall. The mayor of New York City, John Purroy, refused to meet with Bishop Ransome or any members of the coalition. After being rebuffed by the mayor, Bishop Ransome went to Tammany Hall with the group and was promised by Tammany Hall Boss Murphy that he would press for the appointment of a Black man to the New York City police force. However, four years would pass before a Black man would be appointed to the department.

On June 28, 1911, Samuel Jesse Battle became the first Black policeman appointed to the police force since the consolidation of Greater New York. He resided at 255 West 138th Street in Harlem.[12] Battle, while a Red Cap at Grand Central Terminal, studied at night to overcome the handicaps of his lack of a formal education.[13] His appointment to the New York City Police Department in 1911 was at first refused on the grounds that he had a heart murmur. As Battle stated:

. . . that murmur talk didn't seem reasonable to me. I got an examination from the greatest heart specialist in the city. His regular charge was $150, but he reduced his fee to $15 when he heard I was a Red Cap. He gave me a wonderful certificate and my friend sent it to Mayor Gaynor. He took the matter up.[14]

It must be pointed out that this style and method of racial discrimination in the guise of legitimate conduct by the New York City Police Department had been practiced by other city police agencies before this period of time. This has been demonstrated in chapter two when Black men were applying for the position of patrolman in the Brooklyn Police Department. The Black candidates would always undergo a physical examination and a heart checkup by an outside, reputable specialist before undergoing an examination by the police surgeon. This would insure a fair examination and if the results were questionable, the Black candidate would seek a remedy through the courts.[15]

After further difficulties, delays, and examinations, Police Commissioner Waldo came into office. One of his first acts was to appoint Samuel Jesse Battle to the force. After his appointment, Battle was assigned to the West 68th Street station, Manhattan.[16] This assignment was based upon the fact that the west side of Manhattan had seen a substantial increase in the number of Black families living in the area.[17] This resulted in a number of racial incidents and the assignment of Battle to this area was expected to ease the tension in the Black community. This was also a repetition of a similar assignment policy undertaken by the police commissioner of the city of Brooklyn in the 1890s.

Samuel Battle's real trials were only beginning. He faced one of the severest ordeals a man could endure. For more than two years, not one of the white patrolmen spoke a single word to him.[18] As Battle put it, "They did not say anything mean; they did not insult me. Maybe it would have been easier if they had." When word of his hazing by silence reached the newspapers, reporters questioned Battle and his replies were always the same: "I have nothing to say about that, sir. I have no complaints to

make, sir."[19] The hazing by silence treatment that Patrolman
Battle received was again a repetition of the similar conduct by
white policemen of the city of Brooklyn Police Department toward
its new Black patrolmen.

In 1912 Battle, with some other policemen, was assigned to
do some particularly arduous election patrol work. They worked
day and night and had been on their feet for twenty-four hours
when they were at last sent back to the station house to rest.
Battle's comments on this were as follows:

> I was worn out. I sat on a chair, I never went up to the bunk
> room with the others. I just did not like to do it, but this night
> after the others had been upstairs awhile, I was so dead tired,
> I said to myself, "They are probably asleep. I will just slip
> up there and lie across a bed for a little while." Nobody saw
> me come in. I lay on a bed by the door. They were not all
> asleep. Some of them were talking. It was about me, but it
> was too late to sneak out. One of them said, "You know, I'm
> sorry we've treated Battle like this. At first I thought he was
> going to be a rat. But he hasn't said a word, he hasn't made
> a complaint. He attends to his own business. I tell you, he's
> a hell of a good fellow." That made a lot of difference to
> me. . . . After that, everything was all right.[20]

Samuel Battle's display of his attitudes toward the other white
policemen exhibits a type of relationship caused by prejudicial
and discriminating actions he received from the white policemen.
This is based upon the notion that the hated and those who hate
can never be as normal in their attitudes or in their lives as
individuals growing up free from prejudice and discrimination.[21]
Therefore, Battle made the kind of adjustment that was necessary
in order to survive amidst the politically, economically, and
socially dominant group—white policemen.[22]

By the time Battle was transferred to the Harlem police
station located on West 135th Street, in 1913, he was liked and
respected by many of the white officers on the force.[23] Once in
the Harlem community Battle's skill and tact in dealing with

Blacks made him increasingly valuable to his white superiors as well as to the Black community.

In 1919, Battle decided to study for the sergeant's promotional exam. When he applied to the Delehanty School, he was told that a vote on his admission must be taken among all students there. The student body at this institution was totally white. A few days before the vote was taken, there occurred in Harlem the so-called Straw Hat Riots. During the rioting, a white policeman shot and killed a Black man. A group of Blacks closed in on the officer and threatened to lynch him. At the height of the danger, Patrolman Battle appeared on the scene (125th Street and Lenox Avenue) and fought his way through the crowd, rescuing the besieged patrolman. Four days later, when the secret poll was taken at Delehanty School, Battle was endorsed by a unanimous vote.[24]

In 1920, he passed high on the list for sergeant, but Police Commissioner Enright refused to promote him. He had to wait six years until Commissioner McLaughlin, appointed by Mayor Jimmy Walker, promoted him to sergeant.[25] (The position of sergeant was a civil service title and rank which Battle was fully entitled to receive.)

On May 21, 1926, for the first time in the history of the New York City Police Department, a Black man was promoted to the permanent rank of sergeant. There had been a few Black policemen made temporary detective sergeants at various times; however, when Commissioner McLaughlin elevated Samuel Jesse Battle to the rank of sergeant, he set a precedent.[26]

Police Sergeant Battle was assigned to the old 16th Detective Squad as its second-in-command.[27] In 1931, he took the exam for promotion to lieutenant and passed high on the list. As a result, he was appointed to lieutenant in an acting-status on January 7, 1934.[28] Lieutenant Battle was then assigned to the Motor Patrol Unit in Harlem.[29] One year later, January 7, 1935, after Battle's one-year probationary period had ended, he was appointed full lieutenant in the permanent civil service capacity.[30]

Six years later, on Thursday, August 21, 1941, Mayor La Guardia announced at city hall that he would appoint Police

Lieutenant Battle to the office of parole commissioner. The position paid $6000 a year and would expire January 4, 1951. Lieutenant Battle's salary as a police officer, at that time, was $4000 a year.

The appointment of Battle to the position of parole commissioner capped his career in the criminal justice system. His appointment to this position was based upon his record as a police officer and his involvement in social measures independent of the police department. While he was assigned to the Harlem community, which was predominantly Black, he identified himself with many organizations interested in promoting the welfare of Blacks. Each year, for example, he would conduct a one-man campaign to raise funds so that on Thanksgiving Day one thousand underprivileged children, mostly Black, might enjoy turkey dinner and attend a show at one of the Harlem theaters. He had done this work for nineteen years.[31]

In his parole job, Battle specialized in studying the increase in juvenile delinquency in the Harlem community and found ways to assist the various youth of Harlem. Battle served as parole commissioner from 1941 to 1951. Thereupon, he retired from the position.

After his retirement, Battle continued his activities for the Harlem branch of the Young Men's Christian Association. He was involved with summer camps for disadvantaged children, the N.A.A.C.P., the National Urban League, and the United Nations, remaining active until his death.[32] On Saturday, August 7, 1966, at age eighty-three, Samuel Jesse Battle died.[33]

Patrolman Robert H. Holmes, born on July 21, 1888, entered the New York City Police Department on August 25, 1913. He was assigned, for a time, to special detective work and then to the 38th Precinct, located on West 135th Street in Harlem.[34]

At 12:00 A.M., on August 6, 1917, Patrolman Holmes was on duty and assigned to a footpost (Lenox Avenue and 139th Street) when he heard four shots. He ran toward the sound and surprised a burglar climbing out of a window of the first floor of an apartment at 68 West 139th Street. He had been attempting to burglarize the home of one Garfield Rose.[35]

The burglar had fired four shots at Rose, all of which missed, and as the burglar ducked into an alley connecting 139th Street and 138th Street, Patrolman Holmes opened fire by shooting into the air. The burglar responded by shooting twice at the patrolman; however, both bullets went wild. He ran through the alley and took refuge in a hallway. With Holmes in pursuit, the burglar turned and fired two shots which struck their target. The officer received one in the forehead and the other just below the left eye. Before other policemen could arrive at the scene the burglar escaped.

Patrolman Holmes was still breathing when the ambulance arrived, but he expired by the time he reached Harlem Hospital. Thus, on Tuesday morning, August 9, 1917 Patrolman Robert Holmes became the first Black policeman ever killed while on duty in the city of New York.[36]

His was also the first police funeral under a new order requiring that in the case of an officer killed while in the discharge of his duty precinct station flags were to be at half-mast until and during the day of the funeral, with the headquarters flag being half-masted on the day of the funeral. Twenty thousand people lined the streets to pay homage to Holmes on the day of his funeral. Of these, many were Blacks who felt great personal and group loss.[37]

Emanuel Kline was a graduate of Columbia University. He spoke Italian, Spanish, and Chinese fluently. Kline was appointed to the New York City Police Department in 1920.[38] He was promoted to sergeant in 1938 and served as supervisor of patrol in the Harlem community.[39] On January 23, 1947, he was promoted to the rank of acting-captain.[40] He was the first Black to reach the rank of captain in the New York City Police Department, even though it was not a permanent civil service rank.

One month after his appointment, on Monday, February 10, 1947, Acting-Captain Emanuel Kline, while the commanding officer of the Youth Squad in the 6th Division in Harlem, spoke to reporters and indicated that he wanted the public to know that his staff was not Jim Crow. He went on to state that his unit was composed of men with a zeal to assist the Black organizations in stemming crime and other social problems. It must be noted that his staff was composed of fifteen men, many of whom possessed college degrees. This unit was also an integrated one.[41] Kline retired on May 27, 1954, after serving the city of New York and the Harlem community for thirty-four years.[42]

Wesley C. Redding joined the force in 1920. One of Redding's spectacular exploits as a patrolman occurred one night when the young rookie made eight felony arrests singlehandedly. While patroling his beat on Lenox Avenue, he climbed over a grocery store transom and surprised and arrested four burglars. Shortly after booking the quartet at the 135th Street police station, he returned to his beat in time to arrest and disarm four holdup men while in the commission of their crime. For this, he was promoted, by appointment, to the position of detective. Thus, Redding became the first Black to become a New York City police detective. After a long illness, Redding died in 1924.[43]

Reuben Carter, in March 1921, became the first Black officer in the New York City Police Department to be assigned to traffic duty. He was assigned to direct traffic at the intersection of 135th Street and Lenox Avenue.[44]

Louis Chisholm was appointed to the New York City Police Department on March 8, 1921. He was promoted to sergeant on August 8, 1930.[45] He thus became the second Black sergeant in the history of the department. However, he became the first Black sergeant to supervise precinct patrol units of all races.[46]

While a sergeant, Chisholm did a study entitled the "Rising Tide of Crime and Delinquency in Harlem." This research earned him a promotion to acting-lieutenant. He was thereafter assigned to command the Juvenile Aid Bureau at the 135th Street Precinct in Harlem in 1936. Later, he was also given the role of supervisor of the Police Athletic League in the Harlem community.[47]

Nettie B. Harris was appointed to the New York City Police Department on December 29, 1924.[48] Harris is traditionally thought of as having been the first Black woman ever appointed to the force. However, it must be noted that the *Negro Yearbook,* covering the period from 1917 to 1918, indicates that there were

Black women already in the New York Police Department. These women were used as probation officers in connection with the city juvenile courts.[49]

After Harris's appointment to the force, she was first assigned to the Woman's Bureau at city headquarters. In August, 1934, she was transferred to the Crime Prevention Bureau in Harlem.[50] Harris retired from the force in 1951 after serving the Harlem community and the city of New York for twenty-seven years.[51]

George H. Redding was appointed as a patrolman in the New York City Police Department on December 20, 1927.[52] He came to New York City at seventeen from Atlanta, Georgia. He entered the post office department in 1918, working there until his appointment as a patrolman in 1927.[53]

Redding, the younger brother of Wesley Redding, who had already been a member of the New York City Police Department,[54] worked for a year and a half on footpatrol in the Harlem community. When the Crime Prevention Bureau (today known as the Youth Division) was organized in 1929, Redding and four other patrolmen were chosen. He spent nine years working with adolescents.[55]

Redding was promoted to sergeant on April 18, 1939, and to lieutenant on December 20, 1943.[56] As a lieutenant, Redding was assigned to the Gates Avenue Precinct located in Brooklyn.[57] Redding continued his education while a policeman and graduated from City College in June, 1952. Six months later, on January 30, 1953,[58] Redding was promoted to captain. He was the first Black man to reach that rank with a permanent civil service status in the department. Redding was thereupon assigned to the 19th Inspectional Division, at the 80th Precinct, located on Vernon Avenue in Brooklyn.[59] Before the year was out Redding was promoted to deputy inspector (October 16, 1953).[60]

On June 22, 1956, Redding was promoted from deputy inspector to full inspector status. At fifty-five years of age, he assumed command of the 19th Division in the Bedford Stuyvesant section of Brooklyn.[61]

On June 21, 1959, Redding was again promoted. This time

to the rank of deputy chief inspector of the New York City Police Department.[62] He commanded uniformed forces in the east half of Brooklyn.[63]

On Sunday, August 29, 1961, Deputy Chief Inspector George H. Redding died after a long illness while still employed by the department. He was sixty years of age at the time of his death.[64] Redding left a legacy of having been the city's fourth Black police sergeant, the third Black lieutenant, the first Black captain (permanent), the first Black deputy inspector, the first Black full inspector, and the first Black deputy chief inspector.

Benjamin Wallace was appointed to the New York City Police Department in July, 1928.[65] During Wallace's career as an officer, he became known as a friend of the Harlem community and as one of the most decorated Black police officers in the history of the department.

On January 2, 1946, while with a probationary patrolman, Wallace stopped in a bar and grill at 441 Lenox Avenue. He did so in order to question a Raymond Griffiths, a known criminal. When Wallace ordered Griffiths to stand, Griffiths drew a .32 caliber revolver from his coat pocket and fired point blank three times at Wallace. As Griffiths fled to the rear of the premises, Wallace fired five shots, all of them taking effect. Griffiths died instantly. Six days later, Wallace died of his wounds.[66]

Wallace received one of the highest medals that the New York City Police Department can award an officer. On the day of the funeral for Wallace, thousands of Blacks mourned the loss of a friend.[67]

It is important for the reader to be aware of some of the working conditions that Black police officers within the New York City Police Department complained of as being unjust during these years. One of these complaints involved the fact that Black officers were exclusively assigned to work in Black communities. They would not be permitted to work, with rare exception, in the white communities. However, white police officers were permitted to work in both the Black and white communities.

Another objection voiced by the Black police officers was the substantial lack of more Black sergeants and lieutenants on the force. For from 1916 to 1917, other cities led the city of New York in the total number of Black personnel and the number of Black supervisors on the force. One such city was Chicago. It led all other cities in the number of Black policemen.[68] The Black membership of the Chicago Police Department consisted of one lieutenant, ten sergeants, and one hundred and twenty patrolmen,[69] as against, for example, only fifteen Black patrolmen in the New York City Police Department.

The majority of Black police officers in New York were supervised by white police supervisors. Since many of the white police supervisors did not readily accept the Blacks on the force, they in turn acted in such ways as to undermine the presence of Black officers. They did not allow Black and white officers to work together in uniform as patrol teams; Blacks would generally work with each other or by themselves. Black officers received harsher treatment at the hands of white superior ranking officers, a condition which manifested itself in the form of disproportionate amounts of departmental disciplinary action against the Black membership. In addition, Black officers often received the most distasteful working assignments. As a consequence, many Black officers felt slighted and intimidated, creating resentment between the Black and white officers in the department.

This type of behavior would continue to exist in full view of the police commissioners and mayors of New York City who served during this period. Thus, there were two standards of treatment in terms of discipline, assignment, transfer, promotion, and dismissal of white and Black policemen. However, this behavior not only would affect internal relationships, but also would have dire consequences for the relationship between the police and the communities inhabited by Black and Hispanic people.

## NOTES

1. Chambers, *Chronicles of Black Protest,* p. 161.
2. Vann C. Woodward, *The Strange Career of Jim Crow* (Fair Lawn, N.J.: Oxford University Press, 1966), p. 114.

3. Hughes, et al., pp. 264-65.

4. U.S. Department of Commerce, Bureau of the Census, *United States Census of Population: 1920,* Vol. 1, p. 150-51.

5. Emmett Scott, *Official History of the American Negro in World War,* Federal Writers Project, 1919, Washington, D.C., Howard University Library.

6. Hughes, et al., p. 267.

7. Hutchmacher, *A Nation of Newcomers,* p. 88.

8. John Louell, Jr., "Youth Programs of Negro Improvement Groups," *Journal of Negro Education,* 3 (July, 1940): 381.

9. Hughes, et al., pp. 280-81.

10. Benjamin Da Silva, Milton Finkelstein, Arlene Loshin, *The Afro-American in United States History* (New York: Globe Book Co., 1969), pp. 267, 294, 295, 298.

11. "Patrolman's Salaries and Cost of Living Since 1914," Labor Bureau, Inc., 1 Union Square, New York City.

12. Mather, *Who's Who of the Colored Race,* p. 22.

13. *New York Tribune,* 17 July 1931.

14. Ibid.

15. See above, p. 19.

16. *New York Tribune,* 17 July 1931.

17. U.S. Department of Commerce, Bureau of the Census, *Fifteenth Census of the United States,* 1930: Population, 2.98.

18. *New York Post,* 28 June 1938.

19. *New York Tribune,* 17 July 1931.

20. Ibid.

21. Samuel Tenenbaum, *Why Men Hate* (New York: Beechhurst Press, 1947), pp. 169-76.

22. Ibid.

23. *New York Tribune,* 17 July 1931.

24. Ibid.

25. *New York Post,* 28 June 1938.

26. *New York World,* 22 May 1926.

27. *New York Amsterdam News,* 7 May 1966.

28. *New York Age,* 12 January 1935.

29. *New York Sun,* 7 January 1934.

30. *New York Tribune,* 7 January 1935.
31. *New York Post,* 21 August 1941.
32. *New York Times,* 7 August 1966.
33. Ibid.
34. New York City Police Department Historical Files, Alfred J. Young Police Department historian.
35. *New York Post,* 9 August 1917.
36. Ibid.
37. *New York Times,* 9 August 1917.
38. Snelson, n.p.
39. *New York Amsterdam News,* 7 May 1966.
40. *New York Times,* 23 January 1947.
41. *New York Times,* 10 February 1947.
42. "News in Review," *Jet Magazine,* May 1954, p. 10.
43. *New York Post,* 8 July 1956.
44. Snelson, p. 28.
45. Ibid.
46. *New York Amsterdam News,* 7 May 1966.
47. Ibid.
48. Snelson, p. 32.
49. Monroe N. Work, "Negro Policewomen," *Negro Yearbook* (Tuskegee, Ala.: Negro Yearbook Publishing Co., 1918-1919), p. 53.
50. *New York Amsterdam News,* 7 May 1966.
51. Ibid.
52. *New York Post,* 8 July, 1956.
53. Ibid.
54. Ibid.
55. *New York Post,* 14 July 1959.
56. *New York Times,* 6 June 1953.
57. *New York Times,* 2 February 1953.
58. *New York Times,* 30 January 1953.
59. *New York Times,* 2 February 1953.
60. *New York Daily News,* 17 October 1953.
61. *New York Times,* 22 June 1956.
62. *New York Post,* 21 June 1959.
63. *New York Amsterdam News,* 7 May 1966.

64. *New York Times,* 30 August 1961.
65. *New York Amsterdam News,* 7 May 1966.
66. *New York Times,* 3 January 1946.
67. *New York Amsterdam News*, January editions, 1946.
68. Monroe N. Work, "Chicago Leads All Other Cities in the Number of Negro Policemen," *Negro Yearbook* (Tuskegee, Ala.: Negro Yearbook Publishing Co., 1916-1917), p. 41.
69. Ibid.

# IV

## *Black Middle-Management*

Between 1931 and 1950, the third generation of Black police officers entered the New York City Police Department. This generation would witness the continued advancement of the preceding generation of Black officers, for it would be the second generation of Black officers that would be promoted to middle management levels within the New York City Police Department. These officers would represent a substantial number of Black sergeants and lieutenants, of permanent civil service status, in the department.

While Black police officers were making further advancements in the New York City Police Department, this country was, for the first decade, in a depression and two-thirds of Black workers were unemployed. Thus, Black officers had a prestigious economical advantage over other Blacks, as well as many whites in the area of employment.[1]

In 1933, with the election of Franklin Delano Roosevelt to the presidency of the United States, new social, economic, and political programs were initiated. These programs were called the "New Deal." Laws were passed quickly to put men back to work. The government set up numerous programs in which hundreds of thousands of men and boys, many of them Black, were employed in public works projects. This gave some relief to Black Americans who were poorer than ever before.[2]

During this period the sudden outpouring of Negro music, fiction, and poetry, which has been called the Harlem Renaissance, continued. This literary and artistic awakening in the twenties and early thirties has sometimes been referred to as the "Period of Black Renaissance in American Life."[3]

The N.A.A.C.P. and other civil rights groups continued their fight to improve the life of Black citizens in the 1930s. They used the courts most of all. They won some cases; they lost others. One of the most important cases came in 1938 when the Supreme Court ruled that a Black student had the right to enter a state college.[4] The following year World War II began in Europe; on December 7, 1941, the Japanese attacked Pearl Harbor in Hawaii. The United States was in war. In a few days America was also at war with Germany and Italy.

When Afro-Americans entered the armed forces during World War II they found that Black soldiers were segregated. Even officer training schools were segregated.[5] Despite this discrimination, a total of one million Black men and women served this country in World War II,[6] and thousands of Black men gave their lives while in the performance of their duties.[7]

President Roosevelt spoke of the four freedoms for which this country would fight—freedom of speech, freedom of worship, freedom from want, and freedom from fear.[8] Afro-Americans knew what these freedoms meant. They were still trying to get them in their own country.[9] But before World War II ended, Harry S Truman became president of the United States. Recognizing the mistreatment accorded to Blacks in this country while in the service, President Truman ordered equality of treatment and opportunity for all persons in the armed services without regard to race, color, religion, or national origin.[10]

World War II opened new jobs for Afro-Americans in the North. States like New York had passed laws to fight job discrimination although life in the South did not improve. No wonder, then, that millions of Blacks left the South to come to the cities of the North. There they could look for better jobs; there they hoped to find better homes; there, they believed, their children might go to better schools. Life had to be better in the North, because Black political leaders had gained some power in the cities.[11]

When Blacks came from the South to the cities of the North, they found that it was hard to find a place to live, for new buildings had not been put up during the war years. The housing they did find was most often segregated. This was true even of the public housing in New York City. In most cities, Blacks and whites lived in different neighborhoods. When Black people moved into "white" neighborhoods, the whites would move away. Jim Crow did not die, but it was easier to find a job. For one thing, teaching and government service were open, in general, to all of those who had the qualifications. In addition, the growing number of Black voters in the cities meant that Afro-Americans could be elected to public office where they could work to improve life for all Black citizens in the country. In New York, Chicago, Detroit, Cleveland, and other cities, changes were taking place. The center of Afro-American life had moved from farms in the rural South to the big cities of the North.[12]

In 1950, because of the efforts of the N.A.A.P.,[13] the Supreme Court rendered decisions in three cases involving Blacks that weakened the Plessy rule, "separate but equal."[14] This was to set the stage for further changes in the country regarding racial equality in social, economic, and political areas of American life.

Although the "separate but equal" rule established in the courts as legitimate in earlier years was wavering, the New York City Police Department continued a policy of "separate but equal" in its assignment of Black and white personnel to precincts and other commands. This policy with *few* exceptions can be illustrated by the method of promotion and assignment of Black police officers in the department.

In 1931, Samuel Jesse Battle passed the lieutenant's civil service examination. Later that same year, two Black officers were assigned to the motorcycle squad. This was a unit that had never been integrated by the department brass. One of the officers, Gladwell Knowles, was assigned to the Central Park area. The other officer, Charles Williams, was assigned to patrol the Harlem community.[15] On January 7, 1934, Battle was appointed acting-lieutenant and placed in charge of the motor patrol unit in Harlem.[16] In August of that same year, Nettie B. Harris was transferred from a police headquarters' unit to the crime prevention unit in Harlem.[17] On January 7, 1935, Battle was promoted to the permanent civil service rank of lieutenant in the city's police department.[18]

During 1936, Louis Chisholm was also appointed lieutenant, but in an acting-lieutenant capacity.[19] He was assigned to the crime prevention unit in Harlem.[20] In 1938, Emanuel Kline was promoted to the rank of sergeant and then assigned to the Harlem area as a patrol supervisor.[21] One year later, on April 18, 1939, George H. Redding was promoted to sergeant, and assigned to the Juvenile Aid Bureau in Harlem.[22] For approximately ten years, from 1931 to 1941, all of the Black policemen promoted to the rank of sergeant and lieutenant were exclusively assigned to the Harlem area, which had been predominantly populated by Blacks for some years.[23] The Black population in Harlem had risen from 50,000 in 1930 to 215,000 in 1940, an increase of 4.3 times, which composed 90 percent of the entire population of Harlem.

By 1943 there were two Black lieutenants and three Black sergeants. One of the Black lieutenants was Samuel Battle the other, Louis Chisholm. The sergeants were Paul Moore, John Brown, and Emanuel Kline, who was the third Black sergeant on the city's police force. Another sergeant was George H. Redding, who was the fourth Black sergeant on the city's police force.

The east half of Brooklyn had seen a large increase in the Black population. This may have been the reason for the apparent break with the tradition of assigning newly promoted Black sergeants and lieutenants to the Harlem area. This change came when Sergeant Redding was promoted to lieutenant on December 20, 1943. After his promotion, he was assigned to the Gates Avenue Precinct in Brooklyn.[24] Redding, although representative of the second generation, continued to make advancements in the New York City Police Department at the same time third-and-fourth-generation of Black officers were serving the department.

The following paragraphs contain information regarding the third generation of Black police officers in the New York City Police Department.

Eldridge Waith was appointed a policeman on November 21, 1942. In 1947, he was given the designation of detective. For four years, he worked as a member in the 32nd Detective Squad.

In 1953, he was promoted to sergeant and in 1956 he was promoted to lieutenant. Upon reaching the rank of lieutenant, he was once more assigned to the 32nd Detective Squad, this time, however, as its commanding officer.[25]

In July, 1963, Waith became the second permanent-ranked Black captain in the department. Again he was assigned to the detective division. In June of 1965, he was transferred back to the 32nd Precinct in Harlem to serve as its commanding officer, becoming the third Black to command a Harlem precinct.[26] Shortly thereafter, February 25, 1966, Waith was appointed to the rank of deputy inspector, becoming the third Black, again, appointed to that rank. He then served in the 6th Division, which covers the greater portion of Harlem.[27]

In February, 1971, Waith retired from the force as an assistant chief inspector, having served the department for twenty-nine years. Although he was leaving his work in the department, he was not quitting his role in the criminal justice system. For in March of 1971, Waith was appointed commissioner of public safety for the United States in the Virgin Islands and was sent to Charlotte Amalie on St. Thomas.[28]

On Wednesday, July 26, 1972, Waith, after having served as commissioner of the Virgin Islands for eighteen months, accepted a position on the New York City Board of Education. Thus, once again, Waith would be dealing with the perplexing problems of the city as director of safety for the New York City public schools. The appointment of Waith to this position was seen as a method of countering the growing problem of violence in the public school system.[29]

On November 21, 1942, Leslie Carroll was appointed to the New York City Police Department. He became a second-grade detective and one of the most decorated men on the force. Carroll received thirty-seven awards, many of which were for extraordinary acts of bravery. On December 1, 1965, he retired from the force.[30]

Lloyd Sealy was appointed to the New York Police Department on November 21, 1942. Sealy served his first seven years in the 77th Precinct, located in the Bedford-Stuyvesant area of

Brooklyn. In 1949, he was assigned to the Juvenile Aid Bureau. On December 20, 1951, he was promoted to sergeant and returned to uniform patrol in the 77th Precinct.[31] Shortly thereafter, in 1958, he was appointed acting-lieutenant and placed once again in the Juvenile Aid Bureau.[32] On October 26, 1959, he was promoted to lieutenant.[33] While a lieutenant, Sealy became the department's first Black to attend the F.B.I. National Academy (he has since returned as a featured lecturer).[34]

On November 22, 1963, he was promoted to captain and became the third Black to attain this rank.[35] Less than a year later, Sealy became the first Black to command a Harlem precinct.[36] On November 24, 1965, he was appointed deputy inspector and remained in command of the 32nd Precinct in Harlem.[37]

On February 25, 1966, Sealy was promoted to the rank of assistant chief inspector, bypassing the ranks of inspector and deputy chief inspector.[38] This was the first time that any New York police officer in modern times had been lifted to the rank of assistant chief inspector without following the standard procedure of advancement to that rank. After his promotion, Sealy was placed in command of Patrol Borough Brooklyn North,[39] marking not only the first time that a Black man was appointed to the rank of assistant chief inspector, but also the first time a Black man was given a borough command in the New York City Police Department.

On September 9, 1969, Lloyd Sealy retired after having served twenty-eight years on the force. Although he was retiring from the police force, his work in the criminal justice system would continue in the form of a position at John Jay College of Criminal Justice, City University. Sealy became an associate professor in the Criminal Justice Department. The appointment of Sealy to this position was seen as a method of utilizing the vast experience he had obtained while a member of the police department, thus, adding depth to the Criminal Justice Department at John Jay.[40]

Robert Johnson was appointed to the New York City Police Department on January 3, 1946. After completing his training at the police academy, Johnson was assigned to the 32nd Precinct. He worked as a footpatrolman for a few months and was then reassigned to clerical duty in the 10th Division (currently called the 6th Division). Johnson became the first Black officer ever to work in this capacity in the division office. Two years later, in 1948, Johnson was assigned to the plainclothes unit in the 10th Division command. He served in this unit for two years. In 1950 he was assigned to the chief inspector's office for six months. After this assignment, Johnson was returned to the 32nd Precinct. He then worked in uniform, assigned to patrol duties.

In June of 1953, Johnson was promoted to the rank of sergeant. Sergeant Johnson's first assignment was to the 42nd Precinct as a patrol supervisor. Johnson's first assignment made history, for he was the first Black supervisor ever to be assigned to this precinct. Sergeant Johnson remained at the 42nd Precinct for a period of two years. Sometime in 1955, Johnson was assigned to the 43rd Precinct, where he supervised an all-white patrol unit. Johnson's transfer and assignment were based in part on the innovative attitudes that Police Commissioner Francis Adams had undertaken while in office. Thus, it was no mistake that Sergeant Johnson was also the first Black supervisor to be assigned to the 43rd Precinct.

In 1957, Sergeant Johnson was assigned to the 40th Precinct as a patrol supervisor. Johnson served in this command for a period of four years. Then, in 1961, Johnson was reassigned to the 28th Precinct in the same capacity. The following year, in 1962, he was again reassigned, this time to the community relations office in the 6th Division command. One year later, in January of 1963, Johnson was promoted to the rank of lieutenant and remained assigned to the 6th Division.

In 1966, Lieutenant Johnson was sent to the 32nd Precinct as its administrative lieutenant, assigned to desk duties. This marked the first time that a Black lieutenant had ever worked in this capacity in the 32nd Precinct, and it also marked the first time that any Black lieutenant had ever been assigned to the 32nd Precinct.

In June of 1967, Robert Johnson was promoted to the rank

of captain. His first assignment was to the 42nd Precinct as its commanding officer. Johnson again made history, for he was the first Black commanding officer of the 42nd Precinct and the first Black commanding officer in the borough of the Bronx. Captain Johnson remained at the 42nd Precinct for a period of four years. In December, 1971, Johnson was promoted to the rank of deputy inspector, and remained the commanding officer of the 42nd Precinct.

While Deputy Inspector Johnson was in command of the 42nd Precinct, he created the position of "precinct receptionist." This position was held by a civilian and was nonsalaried, its purpose being to bridge the communications gap that existed between some of the community inhabitants and members of the department. The position of precinct receptionist was quickly adapted throughout the entire city police department, for it proved to be a success.

In the spring of 1972, while assigned to the Borough Office of the Bronx, Deputy Inspector Johnson established the first working model of the "Youth Gang Task Force" in the history of the New York City Police Department. It is interesting to note that in 1943 the late Patrolman Holman Bowman of the 32nd Precinct and Patrolman Robert J. Mangum were assigned to the 6th Division as "gang patrolmen." The unit was the first to utilize a "hot-line" telephone number given to television, radio, and other media people. The personnel selected for this detail were picked on the basis of their ability to relate to youths, their working knowledge of the Bronx area, their record on the job, and their observable motivation and incentive to help stem the tide of "street gang violence" in the Bronx. This program instituted by Johnson was highly acclaimed throughout the department and the communities of the Bronx.

In June, 1972, Johnson was promoted to the rank of full inspector and remained assigned to the Bronx borough office. However, in March, 1973, Inspector Johnson was transferred to the 16th Division located in the borough of Queens. This marked another first for Johnson and the department, for Inspector Johnson was placed in charge of the 16th Division, which was the first time that a Black officer was in charge of this division.

Johnson remained assigned to this command for a period of two years.

In April, 1975, Inspector Johnson was transferred to the Bronx field services, placed in charge of Zone 1 as a coordinator for the borough chief. The Zone 1 coordinator covers the South Bronx area.[41] As of this time, Johnson is assigned to the Bronx field services as Zone 1 coordinator.

William R. Bracy was appointed to the New York City Police Department on June 1, 1946. After finishing his training at the police academy, Bracy was assigned as a footpatrolman in the 79th Precinct. Six months later, on January 3, 1947, Bracy was assigned to the youth squad in the 13th Division. Patrolman Bracy's assignment marked the first time that a Black police officer in the New York City Police Department was assigned to a youth squad in the borough of Brooklyn. Patrolman Bracy remained assigned there for two years, working with street gangs in the Bedford-Stuyvesant area. He visited schools and interviewed youths that were involved in situations at these schools and/or neighborhood centers. This was a mixture of police work and social work.

In January, 1949, Bracy was assigned to the plainclothes unit in the public morals section of the 13th Division. Two years later, Bracy was reassigned to the 6th Division plainclothes unit in Harlem. However, on September 30, 1950, five-hundred plainclothes personnel were dropped from their plainclothes assignments throughout the city. As a result, Bracy was transferred to the 79th Precinct in uniform on patrol. While Bracy was assigned to the 79th Precinct, he attended Delehanty School and studied for the promotional exam for sergeant. On October 26, 1954, Patrolman Bracy was promoted to sergeant. Sergeant Bracy was assigned to the 110th Precinct in the borough of Queens. Thus, Bracy became the first Black sergeant to supervise Queens uniform personnel. Bracy was assigned to the 110th Precinct for a period of three and a half years (from October, 1954, to November, 1957). Bracy was assigned from November, 1975, to April, 1958, to the 114th Precinct as a patrol supervisor.

In April, 1958, Sergeant Bracy passed the lieutenant's exam

and was placed on the lieutenant's promotional list. Bracy was then reassigned to the 25th Precinct in the Harlem area of Manhattan. From April of 1958 to October of 1959, Bracy was assigned as a patrol supervisor in the 25th Precinct. He was also placed in charge of warrants from traffic court, and he was also the president of the Guardians Association during this period.

In October of 1959, Bracy was promoted to lieutenant and reassigned to the 19th Precinct as its desk officer, marking the first time ever in the history of the department that a Black police officer was so assigned to the 19th Precinct. Lieutenant Bracy remained there until September, 1961, when he was transferred to the Youth Patrol Bureau, Brooklyn North Youth Squad as its commanding officer. Bracy remained assigned to this unit until April, 1966, when he was assigned to the detective division of the Manhattan North Youth Squad. (At this time the old youth patrol division was incorporated into the detective division.) Bracy was assigned to this unit from April of 1966 to November of 1967. In November, 1967, Lieutenant Bracy made history again when he was assigned to the 101st Division squad as its commanding officer. He became the first Black detective commander in the borough of Queens. Bracy remained assigned until May of 1970, when he was promoted to the rank of captain. After receiving this rank, Captain Bracy was assigned to the 5th Division as a "sho-fly" captain[42] in patrol supervision. Captain Bracy remained in the 5th Division until September, 1970, when he was assigned to the field internal affairs unit in Manhattan North Area.

In March, 1971, Captain Bracy was assigned to the 32nd Precinct as its commanding officer, and in January, 1972, Bracy was promoted to deputy inspector, remaining in command.

In February, 1973, Deputy Inspector Bracy was promoted to full inspector and transferred to the 13th Division as its commanding officer. In May, 1973, the New York City Police Department did away with the divisional commands in each borough, and Inspector Bracy was transferred to the Brooklyn North Area command. In November of the same year, he was promoted again, this time to rank of deputy chief inspector, and assigned to the

Brooklyn North Area command as its executive officer, second in command.[43] In July, 1977, Deputy Chief Inspector William R. Bracy was promoted to assistant chief inspector in charge of the Brooklyn North Area. At the present time he is the highest ranking Black police officer in the department.

Thomas Mitchelson was appointed to the New York City Police Department on September 16, 1946. After completing his training at the police academy, he was assigned to the 48th Precinct as a footpatrolman. Mitchelson served eleven years in general uniform patrol. However, two years, while still a patrolman, were spent in the Police Sports Association, i.e., track and field.

On December 12, 1959, Mitchelson was promoted to the rank of sergeant and assigned to the 81st Precinct. This was an important event, for Sergeant Mitchelson became the first Black patrol supervisor to serve at the 81st Precinct, where he was for a period of three years. In 1962, Mitchelson was assigned to the Brooklyn North Youth Squad as a supervisor and remained in that assignment for two years.

On November 24, 1965, Mitchelson was promoted to the rank of lieutenant. He was thereupon assigned to the 13th Division as a patrol supervisor and desk officer. One month later, he was assigned to the Civilian Complaint Review Board as in investigator, serving the unit for two years. Thereafter, Lieutenant Mitchelson served the following units: six months as a detective supervisor in the 6th Division Detective District; one month as commanding officer, Detective Manhattan North Youth Squad; eighteen months as commanding officer, Narcotics Group 32; two months as a plainclothes supervisor, 6th Division; and one year as the administrative lieutenant in the 32nd Precinct.

On August 6, 1969, Mitchelson was promoted to captain and thereupon made the commanding officer in charge of the 32nd Precinct. Captain Mitchelson commanded the precinct for a period of one and a half years, until March 1, 1971, he was promoted to the rank of deputy inspector and assigned to the Patrol Borough Manhattan North, where he served as an administrator for six months. Deputy Inspector Mitchelson was transferred, but remained in the Manhattan North Area as an administrator in the 6th Division command.

On December 22, 1971, Mitchelson was again promoted, this time to the rank of full inspector. Under this rank, he served as the administrator in the Patrol Borough Manhattan North for three months. He also served as the commanding officer of the 6th Division. The following year, on August 25, 1972, he was promoted to the rank of deputy chief inspector assigned for a period of six months to the 6th, continuing his status as commanding officer.

On March 8, 1973, Mitchelson was promoted again, this time to the rank of assistant chief inspector and placed in the Manhattan North Area command as its commanding officer, the third black officer to receive this distinction. Assistant Chief Mitchelson served in this command with this rank for one year. Then, on January 28, 1974, he became part of history by becoming the first Black New York City police officer to be made a chief of uniform services. The job title itself is the "Chief of Field Services Bureau."[44] Mitchelson retired in July, 1977, because of illness.

Sometime in 1946, Lloyd Gittens joined the New York City police force. One year later, he was assigned to the Manhattan East Youth Squad. In 1951, he was assigned to the 32nd Detective Squad. On July 7, 1955, Gittens became the first Black sergeant to be assigned to the 40th Precinct, in the Bronx, as a patrol supervisor.[45]

Arthur B. Hill joined the New York City Police Department in 1946.[46] In 1959, he was promoted to sergeant and assigned to the South Bronx. In 1961, Hill was promoted to lieutenant. In 1963, he was promoted to captain and returned to the 28th Precinct where he had spent his early years on the force, as its commanding officer. He was the first Black officer to command the 28th Precinct and the second Black to command a Harlem precinct. In 1967, he was advanced to deputy inspector,[47] and two years later he was promoted to inspector and made commanding officer of the 6th Division. Shortly thereafter, Hill was advanced again, this time to deputy chief inspector. By April, 1971, Hill was in charge of the 13th Division in Brooklyn.[48] He remained the commanding officer of the 73rd Precinct until September 3, 1971, when he was transferred to the 13th Division, and assigned as its executive officer.

On September 1, 1972, Arthur B. Hill retired from the New York City Police Department as an assistant chief inspector. Hill was fifty years of age and had served the department for twenty-six years.[49]

John Wilson was appointed to the New York City Police Department on July 1, 1948. Wilson served as a patrolman in the 75th Precinct for a period of nine years. Patrolman Wilson was promoted to the rank of sergeant on November 8, 1957, and assigned to the 32nd Precinct as a patrol supervisor. From March of 1959 to May of 1961, Sergeant Wilson was assigned to the Civil Defense Training Office. On May of 1961, Wilson was assigned to the Police Commissioner's Inspections Squad (P.C.I.S.) under Lieutenant Patrick Murphy (later police commissioner of the New York City Police Department).

On March 30, 1962, Wilson was promoted to the rank of lieutenant, and assigned as a patrol supervisor in the 28th Precinct. However, this assignment lasted for a month, for Lieutenant Wilson was then assigned to the P.C.I.S. Two years later, on June 29, 1964, he was transferred to the Commissioner's Internal Investigation Unit (C.I.I.U.). One year later, sometime in October of 1965, Lieutenant Wilson was again transferred, this time to the Police Commissioner's Investigating Unit (P.C.I.U.). While Wilson was assigned there, he handled investigations of cases involving civilian complaints against members of the New York City Police Department.

In September, 1968, he was transferred to the 81st Precinct as its administrative lieutenant. On November 28, 1968, Wilson was promoted to the rank of captain and became the commanding officer of the 81st Precinct.

On January 13, 1969, Captain Wilson was transferred to the 73rd Precinct. On March 19, 1971, while he was assigned to this command, he was promoted to the rank of deputy inspector.

On March 15, 1972, Deputy Inspector John Wilson was promoted to the rank of full inspector and placed in charge of the 13th Division. One year later, on March 8, 1973, Inspector Wilson was transferred to the Queens detective area as its executive officer. Wilson remained assigned there until February of 1974, when he was transferred to Bronx Area Zone 1 (which is the old 7th Division).[50] On April 28, 1975, Inspector Wilson was transferred to Inspectional Services. He is presently assigned to this unit.

From 1931 to 1950, police-police and police-community contact situations began to be more publicized and politicized. In New York City, in community after community where the Black population was numerically superior, there were complaints of the underrepresentation of Blacks in the police department. Although by January 30, 1935, there were 125 Black officers on the force[51] and by a little more than three years later, there were 147,[52] this did not stay the growing demand by Blacks that the city of New York appoint more Blacks to the department. Besides this complaint of underrepresentation by Blacks, there was the continued complaint of "police brutality."

While Blacks were an inconsequential part of the population of New York City, they passed relatively unnoticed, but the increasing numbers, accompanied by competition for jobs, housing, education and active political power, fueled the fires of racism. Generally speaking, the more Blacks, the sharper the expression of prejudice.

The borough of Brooklyn has seen a continued increase in its number of Black families. It had also witnessed a sharp rise in the number of allegations of police brutality from Blacks regarding their treatment by the white policemen in the New York City Police Department. Hence, on April 29, 1949, Black political groups pressured Mayor O'Dwyer for some affirmative action. The mayor called a press conference in which he outlined the possible solution of this problem. He appointed F. D. Roosevelt, Jr., to head a commission of respected citizens that would investigate the allegations of police brutality against Black citizens. This issue was strengthened by the N.A.A.C.P.'s documentation of the allegations of police brutality in Brooklyn.[53]

While the commission was undertaking the investigation of numerous allegations of police misconduct, three Blacks were killed under circumstances which Black communities thought were "suspicious."[54] The commission promised to get to "the bottom of this" but in the end the Black citizenry of New York City felt that the commission had "whitewashed" the entire matter. This type of action on the part of criminal justice agencies further alienated the Black communities from the police force.[55]

It was also during the late 1940s that Black police officers became increasingly distraught and embittered over the continued mistreatment which they received from the white police officers in the New York City Department. As a result, the Black police officers complained to their Black political leaders, about this problem. The Black leaders responded to the demands that they attempt to change this condition through their political power base. Therefore, they called upon the mayor, the city council, and the police commissioner to intervene in this matter. However, during these years the political responses on the part of the mayors, City Hall and the police department were extremely sluggish.[56] Hence, the discriminatory and prejudicial behavior on the part of the white membership of the department continued to develop unchecked.

One of the complaints by the Black membership of the police department involved the use of white supervisors to supervise the Black police officers on the force. Although there were some Black supervisors on the force (sergeants and lieutenants), they were few in number. Besides this, it must be noted that many of the rising Black supervisors were generally detailed to special assignments within the police department after making an advancement in rank.[57]

In addition to the situation described above, Black police officers were continuing to receive a disproportionate number of disciplinary actions against them from their white supervisors.[58]

There were other examples of the existence of two separate

and unequal behavioral systems within the police department. This was evident in the type of assignments that Black police officers were excluded from, in general, within the department. Assignment to certain "sensitive positions" in the detective bureau[59] was given primarily to white officers. Even when Black police officers were assigned to the detective bureau, it would be too often on the basis of some spectacular arrest in which the officer risked his or her life.[60] This, however, was not the case when it came to the assigning of white police officers to similar positions. Many of these white officers had relatives or friends on the force who would "look out for them," and, in general, assignments were in the hands of the white higher-ranking officers on the force. To add to this dilemma, the internal advancements—from the lowest rank of detective, third grade, to the highest rank, first grade—were also ethnic in nature and given in part to those Blacks who "curried the favor" of their white supervisors. More often than not, the Black detective would remain in a particular detective rank for a longer period of time than his white counterpart. It would take, again, a spectacular arrest of an infamous character or the solving of a particularly perplexing case to catapult the Black officer into a higher position within the Detective Bureau.[61]

The uniformed services were not exempt from the same type of discriminatory practice as found in the detective bureau. For during this period (from approximately 1931 to 1950), the practice of assigning Black police officers to predominantly Black and Hispanic communities continued. This was a policy, which was pointed out earlier in this study, that had its roots dating back to the 1890s. Thus, many Black police officers were still wondering when their chance would come to work in the white communities, the same way that white officers worked in Black and other minority communities.

The exemption of Black officers from certain select detective units had a parallel in the uniformed services. Black uniformed police officers were not assigned to "special uniformed details.[62] However, there were more Blacks assigned to the detective bureau than to "special units" within the uniformed services during this period of time.

The Guardians Association was an official organization not recognized by the department from 1943 to 1949. During this time, Robert J. Mangum served as president. Mangum made two requests for official recognition to Commissioners Valentine and Wallander, which were both denied. In 1949 a third request was made to Police Commissioner William O'Brien. Contacts were made by Mangum with Adam Clayton Powell, Jr., and J. Raymond Jones, the two leading Black political figures at that time. Through their efforts with then Mayor William O'Dwyer and Police Commissioner William O'Brien, official recognition was attained. Robert J. Mangum is presently a judge in the Court of Claims, State of New York.[64]

The Guardians Association would play a dominant role in the further advancement of Black police officers on the force. Their role would not be confined to merely this period. For in the years to follow, the Guardians would do much toward furthering the cause of "racial justice," not only in the New York City area but on a national and international basis via involvement in political protest in other states, and in international meetings involving other police officers from foreign countries.[65]

By 1950, there were 368 Black police officers in the New York City Police Department. It is true that this figure represents a substantial increase over the 125 in 1935, and the 147 in 1938, however, Blacks were still underrepresented,[66] for the statistical information contained in the 1950 census reveals that the percentage of Blacks in the city was more substantial than that on the force.[67]

## NOTES

1. Rene A. Wormser, *The Story of the Law* (New York: Simon & Schuster, 1962), p. 441.
2. Ibid., p. 448.
3. Woodward, p. 125.

4. Da Silva, et al., p. 294.
5. Chambers, pp. 174-76.
6. Da Silva, et al., p. 295.
7. Hughes, et al., pp. 294-95.
8. *New York Times, New York Post, New York Daily News,* 7-14 December 1941.
9. N.A.A.C.P., "Letter to President Roosevelt," *Crisis,* Vol. 48 (1941): 71, 72, 81, 83, 85.
10. Da Silva, et al., p. 298.
11. Huthmacher, p. 84.
12. U.S. Department of Commerce, Bureau of the Census. The statistical figures on the increases in the total Black population in the northern cities are reflected in the 1930, 1940, and 1950 U.S. Census.
13. Milton L. Barron, *American Minorities* (New York: Alfred A. Knopf Co., 1962), p. 214.
14. Huthmacher, p. 81.
15. *Amsterdam News,* 7 May 1966.
16. *New York Sun,* 7 January 1934.
17. *New York Amsterdam News,* 7 May 1966.
18. *New York Tribune,* 7 January 1935.
19. Snelson, p. 34
20. *New York Amsterdam News,* 7 May 1966.
21. Ibid.
22. *New York Times,* 18 April 1939.
23. Handlin, *The Newcomers,* p. 49.
24. *New York Times,* 20 December 1943.
25. *New York Times,* 19 June 1965.
26. Ibid.
27. *New York Times,* 27 July 1972.
28. *New York Times,* 26 July 1972.
29. Ibid.
30. *New York Amsterdam News,* 14 May 1966.
31. *New York Times,* 20 December 1951.
32. *New York Amsterdam News,* 14 May 1966.
33. *New York Times,* 26 October 1959.
34. *New York Amsterdam News,* 14 May 1966.

35. *New York Times,* 22 November 1963.
36. *New York Times,* 24 August 1964.
37. *New York Post,* 24 November 1965.
38. *New York Times,* 25 February 1966.
39. Ibid.
40. *New York Times,* 9 September 1969.
41. Material obtained from a personal interview with Inspector Robert Johnson, August, 1975.
42. "Sho-fly" captain—one who is not in a commanding officer capacity, but is treated as a captain without a ship. He is usually responsible for disciplining the personnel assigned to a divisional district. Hence, he generally develops and lodges departmental charges and specifications against members of the department.
43. Material obtained from a personal interview with Deputy Chief Inspector William R. Bracy, July, 1975.
44. Material obtained from a personal interview with Chief of Field Services, Thomas Mitchelson, July, 1975. Chief Mitchelson retired July 22, 1977.
45. *Chicago Defender,* 9 July 1955.
46. *New York Times,* 28 July 1969.
47. Ibid.
48. *New York Times,* 18 April 1971.
49. *New York Times,* 1 September 1972.
50. Material obtained from a personal interview with Full Inspector John Wilson, June, 1975.
51. *New York Post,* 30 January 1935.
52. *New York Post,* 28 June 1938.
53. *New York Times,* 29 April 1949.
54. *New York Times,* April, May, June, 1949.
55. *New York Times,* 29 April 1949.
56. *New York Times,* April, May, and June, 1949.
57. This attitude on the part of Blacks was manifested in the newspapers and periodicals published in and around the New York area. (*Jet, Sepia, Age, World, Carrier, Afro,* etc.)
58. Ibid.
59. Black police officers were not present in the following units:

Intelligence Unit, Bomb Squad, Pickpocket and Confidence Squad, and a few other specialized units.

60. As of June 28, 1938, there were eleven Black detectives on the New York City Police Department. All of them had outstanding arrest records. (*New York Post* 28 June 1938).

61. This information was obtained by surveying the newspapers for information on the appointments of Blacks to detective. Information was also obtained through interviews with retired Black New York City Police Officers.

62. Black officers were excluded from the following units: Aviation Unit, Early Forensic Unit, and Emergency Service, and there were very few Black officers assigned to the mounted units and the motorcycle squads.

63. Materials obtained from personal interviews with present and retired Black police officers, January 1975-December 1976.

64. Guardians Association Conference, April 5, 1975, guest speaker Hon. Robert Mangum.

65. *New York Times,* 10 March 1973.

66. U.S. Department of Commerce, Bureau of the Census, *United States Census of Population:* 1950, *Characteristics of the Population.*

67. Ibid.

# V

## The Black Hierarchy

From 1951 to 1970, the fourth generation of Black New York City police officers joined the force. They, like their predecessors, would witness the continued advancement of the preceding generations of officers. During this period, it would be the third generation of Black officers who would acquire some of the highest positions within the New York City Police Department. Some of the third-generation officers would become the first Black officers to command precincts, divisions, and even boroughs.

While as police officers in New York City, both generations of Black officers would experience the impact of historic events—both on the national and local scenes. These events would foster substantial changes in the social, economic, and political way of life in America.

One of the most important changes in America came in 1954, in the case of *Brown* v. *the Board of Education.*[1] The Supreme Court ruled in this case that the "separate but equal"[2] ruling by an earlier court was not allowed by the Constitution of the United States. The court ruled that "separate" schools were "unequal," therefore unconstitutional and illegally producing an inferior level of education for Blacks. At last the Constitution was "color blind"! The court waited a year; then it ordered that all schools in the country be desegregated quickly.

The South, and some northern areas of the country, fought against the implementation of this ruling. They would not give up white control over Black life.[3] Hence, during the 1950s, two forms of political reaction to this white resistance to "law and order" became the weapons of Black groups and their white friends in their fight for equal rights. One of these forms was the use of nonviolent protests, the other was the use of civil disobedience.[4]

During this period, Blacks turned toward peaceful open meetings, usually in Black churches. Blacks refused to obey laws which they felt were "unjust." They instituted boycotts against businesses that followed Jim Crow policies. One of the best known boycotts took place in Montgomery, Alabama. It lead to the rise of the late Reverend Dr. Martin Luther King, Jr., as a new Black leader.[5]

Groups like the Congress of Racial Equality, the N.A.A.C.P., the National Urban League, the Southern Christian Leadership Conference, and others led the civil rights movement in the United States during the 1950s and early 1960s.[6] Although "nonviolence"[7] was practiced in many forms, "sit-ins" and "freedom-riders" were the forms that gained international notoriety. In some places in the North and South, whites agreed to end some kinds of discriminatory practices. In other places, however, the law of the land was met with stiff resistance and the Congress and the President of the United States had to bring the powers of national government to bear upon those who prevented the implementation of the law.[8]

It seemed that all the rulings of the Supreme Court and all the laws of the country would not end Jim Crow. The millions of Afro-Americans in this country would have to do the job themselves. They would have to become voters and then use the power of their votes to change life in their particular parts of the country.[9] It was clear to many Blacks that the right to vote was one of the essentials in the recipe for social, economic, and political change in this country. Hence, thousands of Black and white citizens came to those areas of the country, mainly the South, that needed reexamination of the political status of Blacks. As a result, these same people participated in voter registration drives. They also instructed Blacks how to use their voting power. Despite a great deal of interference by local and national organizations against the voter drive for Blacks, many Black citizens began to participate in the electoral process in this country. The price for this "freedom," and many other freedoms that were basically shared by whites, was enormous. Acts of violence against civil rights advocates continued and in time even were accelerated in their barbarity. Numerous churches were bombed or burned to the ground, sometimes resulting in the death of innocent Black children. There were beatings and even shootings of Black and white civil rights activists. Several incidents resulted in the deaths of notable civil rights leaders.[10]

By 1964, the nonviolent movement had been attacked by white racists to such an extent that many younger Blacks began to question the use of peaceful methods to acquire basic rights under the law, and some turned to new leaders and new groups who espoused the use of force to meet force in order "to carve out a place for themselves in the political social order."[11] Although ten years of nonviolent protest had weakened Jim Crow, other problems still remained as Black citizens continued their drive for equality in fact as well as in the stated laws of the land.

For some Blacks, real gains had been made by the middle of the 1960s. Studies made by the federal government showed the areas in which Blacks had achieved success. Two out of every five poor Black families were no longer poor. There were more Afro-American doctors, lawyers, dentists, engineers, teachers, businessmen and women, and craftsmen and women. More than half the country's Black population had moved to cities in the North. Cities like New York showed a substantial gain in their Black population.[12] There had also been a growth in the number of Black policemen and policewomen in the northern cities. This was exemplified in a number of cities, two of which were Washington, D.C., and New York City.[13]

Although the gains previously mentioned were a welcome advantage for Blacks in general, millions of Blacks had not yet improved their lives. For the same studies that showed how life for Blacks had improved also showed how much further they still had to go. More Black students than white students dropped out of high school. Even when Black students completed high school, fewer of them, in comparison to white students, would be able to attend college.[14] To add to this problem, when a Black college graduate earned a similar degree as his white counterpart, he would earn less with the same credentials. In this respect he was not unlike other Blacks in the employment field. Many Black workers earned less than whites doing the same kind of work.[15] More Blacks lived in real poverty; fewer had full-time jobs. In most large cities, more Blacks lived in the areas of the city that were substandard in housing, educational facilities, and general conditions of life.[16] Blacks living in such conditions would read the paper, watch television, and see programs that showed how the middle-class white family lived. Blacks would ask why they could not participate in their country's great wealth.[17] The younger Blacks knew that they were a little better off than their parents had been, but they wanted more. Their aspirations and hopes decreed a more substantial change in this country's treatment of its Black citizenry.[18] Yet, they had little hope that things would ever change for them. The dreams that began with the New Deal[19] had not come true. As a result, some Blacks feared that the work done by the older Black organizations could not bring them full "equality under the law."[20] Therefore, they turned to more militant groups that promised the way toward a better life.[21]

Groups like the Black Muslims, the Congress of Racial Equality (C.O.R.E.), and Student Nonviolent Coordinating Committee (S.N.C.C.) began to espouse two concepts: "Black Power" and "Black Nationalism."[22] "Black Power" is a demand that Black Americans have responsible participation in the decision-making process and in the administration of the significant affairs which affect themselves and the whole society.[23] "Black Nationalism" expresses the idea that Black people are better than whites. Blacks should not mix with whites. Although integration has long been the goal of most civil rights groups, it was not a goal of groups like the Black Muslims. This group, and others like it, expressed the concept of sovereignty—a Black nation within the United States.[24] Since this period some of these groups have substantially changed their respective positions.

Many Blacks and whites in America were so accustomed to seeing power in the hands of white people they could not understand the notion of Blacks' sharing power with whites. Nor could they accept the concept that Blacks could wield power responsibly.[25] This fear was evident in the New York City Police Department. The department did not feel that Black police officers could effectively supervise precincts, let alone divisions and boroughs. It was not until the rise of Black Power and Black Nationalism, pride in self and group, that the cohesive efforts of Blacks produced tremendous changes in the department. These changes were basic to the American way of life. This country's progress in economic, social, technological, and cultural fields has been stimulated and expanded by pressure groups. Therefore, political pluralism has contributed to America's greatness.[26]

On June 3, 1963, President Johnson warned that there was going to be trouble in the large cities across the nation unless something was done about the economic, social, educational, housing, and other substandard conditions in which the majority of Blacks in the country were living.[27] However, his warnings went unheeded by the Congress and other governmental agencies throughout the nation. One year later, during the summer of 1964, a riot erupted in Harlem. It suggested a pattern of racial explosions that would repeat themselves in city after city across the country. This produced the reference to summer months in those cities with large Black populations as "long hot summers."[28]

In the summer of 1965, a riot in Watts, a Black community of Los Angeles, carried a death total of thirty-five. There were 883 persons injured and 3,598 persons arrested. Fire damage came to $175,000,000 and property losses exceeded $46,000,000. The Watts riot, like that occurring in Harlem a year earlier, was ignited by the Black community's resentment with what it felt to be the gross mistreatment of Black citizens by white policemen.[29]

There were also major riots in Chicago and Cleveland in 1966, in Newark and Detroit in 1967, and in Washington, D.C., and Cleveland in 1968.[30] In a sense, these riots represented a Black response to what was interpreted as white provocation. The underlying causes, however, were much deeper than the incidents that brought thousands of Black citizens into the streets to be confronted by thousands of police and national guardsmen.[31]

A commission of distinguished Americans, appointed by President Johnson, investigated the causes of the riots. The National

Advisory Commission on Civil Disorders (Kerner Commission) found that the police were in part responsible for the very disorders they were called upon to control. Relations between the police and minority groups were found to be a major source of grievance, tension, and, ultimately, disorder.[32]

The Kerner Commission listed a number of ghetto grievances, with police harassment and brutality high on the list. Police brutality was defined as physical and verbal abuse. Witnesses told the commission that police actions stripped Blacks of their dignity. A University of Michigan professor testified that nearly half of all police officers in a city he studied showed extreme prejudice. They described Blacks and their communities as "animals" and the "animal kingdom" or as a "zoo."[33] This type of attitude, on the part of white police officers, was also present in the New York City Police Department.

As a result of the Kerner Commission report, numerous new and dramatic programs by the federal government were instituted.[34] Many of these programs were labeled as "affirmative-action policies" by those agencies affected, as well as by the news media. These policies, discussed below, had a direct effect on the hiring, assignment, and promotion policies of the New York City Police Department with regard to Black and Hispanic police officers.

Blacks in the department had made substantial gains prior to the Supreme Court decision of 1954, and the third generation of Black police officers had been responsible for establishing a number of "firsts." The following paragraphs represent some of the important accomplishments of the third generation during this period.

Sometime in 1951, Lt. Charles Jones became the first Black officer to command a precinct detective squad. He was placed in charge of the 28th Precinct Detective Squad located on 123rd Street in Harlem.[35] On January 1, 1953, Jones was transferred from the 123rd Street station to the Sheriff Street station. There he was placed in charge of the detective squad at that precinct.[36]

On August 23, 1951, William Leon Rowe became the first Black appointed to one of the top-ranking positions in the New

York City Police Department. Rowe was appointed to the rank of 7th deputy commissioner.[37] As a commissioner, he served as coordinator for the department on community problems on a city-wide basis. He was instrumental in paving the way toward a more complete integration of personnel within the New York City Police Department.[38]

Sometime in 1952, Lt. Robert J. Mangum, the only Black commanding officer in the Bronx, was placed in charge of the Juvenile Aid Bureau—the first time a Black commanded a unit that included white policewomen.

On January 1, 1953, Lt. Carl A. Jordan was promoted to acting captain. He was the second Black to achieve this rank on the New York City Police Department. He was given the opportunity to be the first supervisor in the department to head the newly formed detective unit at the West 54th Street station. Jordan had been attached to the Manhattan East detective headquarters.[39]

On December 16, 1953, Dr. R. S. Wilkinson became the second Black police surgeon.[40] The first Black police surgeon was Dr. Louis T. Wright, later to be the president of the board of directors of the NAACP. The importance of his appointment to such a position in the police department is that rarely were Black doctors recognized as experts in their fields by a large consensus of the white population. It must also be pointed out that many of the Black candidates who applied for the position of police officer were all too often discriminated against in their examinations by the medical staff of the department. Therefore, this appointment can be viewed as an effort to alleviate this problem with regard to the recruitment of Black officers. Today the department has a Black chief surgeon, Dr. Clarence Robinson.

After the Supreme Court decision of 1954, it appears that a number of Black police officers in the department were advanced in rank and place in assignments that required command decisions. Whether or not the advancements were directly related to a shift in the racial thinking of the country is hard to prove conclusively. However, the promotions and assignments were impressive firsts for the department and for those Blacks who experienced this obvious change of heart on the part of the higher-ups.

On October 26, 1954, Police Officer William R. Bracy was promoted to the rank of sergeant. Thereupon, he was assigned to the 110th Precinct as a patrol supervisor of uniformed personnel. Sergeant Bracy thus became the first Black to supervise personnel in the borough of Queens.[41] Three years later, in November of 1957, Bracy was transferred to the 114th Precinct and thereby became the first Black to supervise personnel at that precinct.[42]

While Sergeant Bracy's promotion and assignment is representative of the third generation of Black police officers on the force, there were important firsts made by the fourth generation of Black officers. As a matter of fact some of this history made by fourth-generation Black officers was accomplished while they were still assigned to the police academy. This change is exhibited by one Black officer in the following paragraph.

In May of 1955, Police Officer Manuel Jackson became the first Black officer to receive the Bloomingdale Trophy. Jackson earned the highest academic average while a probationary officer in the New York City Police Academy. He achieved a 90.76 average over 735 other officers in his graduating class. The award was presented by the department store owner Lyman Bloomingdale while Police Commissioner Francis Adams and Mayor Robert F. Wagner offered congratulations.[43]

On June 22, 1956, George H. Redding, representing the second generation of Black officers, was promoted to full inspector. He was placed in command of the 19th Division in the Bedford-Stuyvesant area of Brooklyn.[44] Thus, three generations of Black police officers showed advancement, each on its own level.

It was not by chance that a Black police officer won an award for the display of his academic abilities. For there were important changes occurring in the New York City Police Department. More and more, police officers began attending colleges and universities in and around the city. Thus, there was a marked increase in the number of police rookies with college backgrounds and even college degrees.[45] This increase was also present among some of the Black officers in the city's police department.[46]

It would be under these circumstances that the fourth generation of Black police officers would enter the police force. They would witness a continued advancement of the third generation of Black officers in the department. Some of these officers of the third generation would set examples for the fourth generation to follow. In fact, much of the material obtained, through personal interviews of members of both generations, seems to add credibility to this statement.

The next few pages will profile the careers of Black officers who have added to the firsts made by Blacks, as well as to the depth of Black knowledge and experience in law enforcement.

Charles Henry joined the New York City Police Department on June 15, 1951. Henry was fifth on the list that contained five thousand names. Patrolman Henry had prior experience as a police officer with the New York Port Authority before joining the city police force.

After completing the training at the police academy, Patrolman Henry was assigned to the 81st Precinct on foot-patrol. He remained assigned there for a period of seven and a half years. On February 26, 1958, he was promoted to the rank of sergeant and assigned to the 28th Precinct as a patrol supervisor. On April 7, 1958, Sergeant Henry was assigned to the 79th Precinct, where he remained as a patrol supervisor for four years. Then on March 30, 1962, he was promoted to the rank of lieutenant and assigned to the 23rd Precinct. A few months later, he was transferred to the 2nd Division as a patrol supervisor and shortly thereafter, was transferred to the youth division. Henry remained assigned to this unit for approximately two and a half years. On March 30, 1965, he was transferred to the Deputy Commissioner of Community Relations unit. While assigned there, Lieutenant Henry worked on solving community problems in the Brooklyn North Area.

On June 9, 1966, he was again transferred, this time to the Civilian Complaint Review Board. Two months later, he was transferred to the 75th Precinct as a desk officer. Henry had passed the captain's exam and there was unrest in the 75th Precinct by a large number of Black residents regarding social problems, some of which were related to the police department.

On August 17, 1967, Lt. Charles Henry was promoted to the rank of captain and assigned to the 79th Precinct as its commanding officer. Two years later, on June 5, 1969, he was promoted to the rank of deputy inspector. Later that year, Deputy Inspector Henry was transferred to the 7th Detective District as its administrative aide. Then on May 29, 1970, he was transferred to the 12th Division and placed in charge of its uniformed personnel.

On November 24, 1971, Henry was transferred again, this time to the personnel bureau. While he was assigned there, he became involved in a recruitment drive for Black and Hispanic officers for the New York City Police Department. The success of the drive became apparent in the increased numbers of Blacks and Hispanics on the civil service list for the position of police officer in 1973. On January 26, 1973, Deputy Inspector Henry was transferred again, this time to the employment division, as its commanding officer. While Henry was assigned there, he was in charge of the investigations of prospective candidates for the position of police officer.

On July 9, 1973, Deputy Inspector Henry was transferred to the Bronx Area Field Service and placed in charge of the community affairs aspect of that command. On May 10, 1974, he was transferred to the 103rd Precinct as its commanding officer. On April 28, 1975, he was promoted to full inspector and transferred to Queens Area Field Service as a field control inspector, Zone 3, where he is presently assigned.[47]

Hamilton Robinson was appointed to the New York City Police Department on March 1, 1954. Robinson's first assignment came before he finished his training at the police academy; he was assigned to the Chief Inspector's Office where he worked as an invesitgator in plainclothes. In June of 1954, Robinson returned to the police academy and completed the requirements in September, 1954.

Robinson was then assigned to footpatrol, first in the 25th

Precinct and then in the 24th. Two years later he was transferred again, this time out of the borough of Manhattan, to the 90th Precinct in the northern area of Brooklyn. While Robinson was assigned to this command, he worked two years as a "124-man."[48] On July 31, 1963, he was promoted to sergeant and assigned to the 83rd Precinct as a uniform patrol supervisor. In April, 1965, he was assigned to the inspections division.

On October 13, 1966, Robinson was promoted to lieutenant. In October of 1969, he was transferred to the Manhattan North Area command, and placed in charge of a special squad named the Preventive Enforcement Patrol unit, generally known as P.E.P. This was an experimental unit which was composed of minority New York City police officers working in both uniform and plainclothes. The P.E.P. unit was made-up of these officers who went through the cadet program at the New York City Police Academy. Although the unit was highly successful in many respects (arrests and convictions), and shared the esteem of the Black and Hispanic community, the unit received adverse publicity and harassment from members of the department. As a result, the unit was disbanded in December, 1971 and Lieutenant Robinson was transferred to the 6th Division and assigned as a patrol supervisor of uniformed personnel.

On March 15, 1972, Robinson was promoted to the rank of captain and assigned to the 28th Precinct as its executive officer. On November 20, 1972, he was made its commanding officer. On December 22, 1972, he was promoted to deputy inspector. On May 1, 1975, Deputy Inspector Robinson was transferred to the Manhattan North Area, Zone 3, where he is presently assigned.[49]

Glanvin Alveranga was appointed to the New York City Police Department on November 1, 1955. However, Alveranga had prior police experience with the New York Port Authority. He worked for the Port Authority for three and a half years.

After Alveranga completed his training as a New York City police rookie officer, in February, 1956, he was assigned as a footpatrolman in the 25th Precinct. Three years later, he was assigned as an investigator in the Juvenile Aid Bureau, Unit 5, of the 40th Precinct, located in the South Bronx.

In December of 1962, Patrolman Alveranga was promoted to the rank of sergeant and assigned to the 20th Precinct as a patrol supervisor. The following year, 1963, he was transferred to the planning bureau, which was part of the police commissioner's office. While he was assigned there, he worked on ways of improving the efficiency of the department. In September, 1964, Sergeant Alveranga was transferred to the police academy as an instructor. In December, 1967, he was promoted to the rank of lieutenant and remained assigned to the police academy. However, from June of 1967 to October of 1967, he was assigned to the 42nd Precinct as a patrol supervisor.

In March, 1969, Lieutenant Alveranga was transferred to the 88th Detective Squad and made its commanding officer. In June of 1972, with the introduction of specialization throughout the New York City police force, he was transferred to the Brooklyn borough office and assigned as an aid to the borough commander.

In August of 1972, Alveranga was promoted to the rank of captain and assigned to the 103rd Precinct as its executive officer, becoming its commanding officer in March, 1973. Later that same year, he was promoted to the rank of deputy inspector.

In May, 1974, Deputy Inspector Alveranga was assigned to the Brooklyn South Area as an aide to the Zone 3 commander, where he is presently.[50]

Richard McBride was appointed to the New York City Police Department on February 1, 1955. After graduating from the police academy, he was assigned to footpatrol at the 110th Precinct, Queens. In April, 1958, McBride was transferred to the 6th Division plainclothes unit, working two years in this command.

In September, 1963, McBride was promoted to the rank of sergeant and assigned to the 10th Precinct. He worked as a patrol supervisor for a period of three years. Then he was transferred to the Queens Youth Squad as a supervisor for all of the Queens area youth squad personnel, the first Black to command this unit.

In May, 1967, Sergeant McBride was promoted to the rank of

lieutenant and assigned to the Bureau of Special Service for a period of seven months, after which he was assigned to the 5th Detective District as a detective supervisor. One year later, in November of 1968, he was assigned to the 103rd Detective Squad as its commanding officer. Thus history was made in the New York City Police Department, for Lieutenant McBride became the second Black detective squad commander in the borough of Queens.

On December 31, 1971, the precinct detective squads were abolished and the implementation of specialization unfolded throughout the entire police department. Lieutenant McBride was thereupon transferred to the 16th Homicide Detective Zone. In April, 1974, McBride was promoted to the rank of captain. He was subsequently transferred to the Brooklyn South Area as its executive officer in charge of the 72nd Precinct. Later that same year, he was transferred to the Brooklyn South Area as a zone coordinator of Detective District 11. In 1977 he was transferred to the 73rd Precinct as its commanding officer.[51]

DeForest Taylor was appointed to the New York City Police Department on February 20, 1956. Upon completing his training at the police academy Patrolman Taylor was assigned to the 87th Precinct in the communications and records division. Taylor remained in this unit for approximately eight years.

On November 26, 1965, Patrolman Taylor was promoted to the rank of sergeant and assigned to the 71st Precinct as a patrol supervisor of uniformed personnel, where he remained assigned until October of 1968, when he was assigned to the chief of detective's special unit under the Bureau of Special Service, where he worked on confidential cases and supervised personnel involved in similar work.

On August 6, 1969, Taylor was promoted to the rank of lieutenant and assigned to the 13th Division. Lieutenant Taylor was a plainclothes supervisor in the 13th Division for two and one half months. In October he was transferred to the 80th Precinct and assigned as its desk officer. In August of the following year, he was assigned to the 6th Division in Upper-Manhattan as a supervisor of plainclothes personnel. In November of 1971,

Taylor was transferred to the 81st Precinct as its operations officer. In April of 1972, Lieutenant Taylor was transferred to the Civilian Complaint Review Board as an investigator. On October 27, 1972, Taylor was promoted to captain and thereupon assigned to the 79th Precinct as its executive officer.[52] In September, 1975 Captain Taylor was transferred to the 28th Precinct as its commanding officer. On August 15, 1977, he was promoted to deputy inspector and transferred to the Brooklyn North Area as a zone coordinator.

By February of 1956, there were 1,031 Black police officers in the New York City Police Department.[53] In addition to this figure, there were 31 Black police sergeants on the force in April of 1958.[54]

Toward the close of the 1950s Blacks continued to make advancements in the city's police department. On June 21, 1959, George H. Redding, representative of the second generation, was promoted to the rank of deputy chief inspector. This was the first time that any Black police officer in the history of the department achieved this rank. Deputy Chief Inspector Redding also became the first Black officer to command the eastern half of the borough of Brooklyn.[55] Then, in October, 1959, Sergeant William Bracy, representative of the third generation, was promoted to the rank of lieutenant and assigned to the 19th Precinct as its desk officer. This was the first time in the history of the police department that a Black officer supervised the 19th Precinct in this capacity.[56] And, on December 12, 1959, Thomas Mitchelson was promoted to sergeant and assigned as a patrol supervisor in the 81st Precinct. This was the first time that a Black supervisor was assigned to the 81st Precinct. Sergeant Mitchelson was also representative of the third generation of Black police officers in the department.[57]

Nonetheless, by the end of the 1950s, tension had risen to uneasy levels in the Black areas of New York City. The majority of Blacks living in the city were residing in large concentrations in certain sections of New York. The 1960 census revealed that there were 1.1 million Blacks living in New York City, 400,000 in Harlem, and 300,000 in Bedford-Stuyvesant in Brooklyn. The third largest concentration of Blacks was in the South Bronx. These areas of the city would become focal points of Black protest and turbulence.[58]

On July 13, 1959, an incident involving five hundred Blacks in the Harlem community erupted as the result of two white police officers' being accidently shot. In response to this incident, Police Commissioner Kennedy sent hundreds of extra officers (white) into the Harlem community.[59] The reaction of the people of Harlem was dismay and shock. Reports of a possible "police state" echoed throughout the Harlem community.[60] James Baldwin reflected on this policy when he stated:

> . . . there are few things under heaven more unnerving than the silent, accumulating contempt and hatred of a people. He [the white police officer] moves through Harlem, therefore, like an occupying soldier in a bitterly hostile country; . . . The white policeman, standing on a Harlem street corner, finds himself at the very center of the revolution now occurring in the world.[61]

As a result of this policy on the part of the police commissioner, various Black political organizations in Harlem took their complaints to Mayor Wagner. On August 19, 1959, the mayor created the Commission on Harlem Affairs under Deputy Mayor O'Keefe's authority. The establishment of this commission was viewed by many New Yorkers as a method of cutting down on the racial tension in the Harlem community.[62]

The commission probed the complaints of the Harlem residents and reported back to the mayor. They indicated a need for substantial changes in the areas of housing, education, employment, and law enforcement.[63] However, the complaints of Blacks continued to increase in the city of New York against the police department. This was a prime indicator of the ineffectiveness of the New York City Police Department. The department did not gain and maintain the confidence of the citizens in its community. Thus its effectiveness was curtailed and its integrity and ability questioned.

Public trust in and support of a police department can be obtained only when citizens are confident that it will not overstep safeguards of individual liberty and when individual policemen demonstrate that they are interested in and actively engaged in promoting the public peace and welfare.[64] The police commissioner, realizing that the New York City Police Department, as an agency, must be able to project to the citizens of the community its ability and willingness to serve with integrity and effectiveness, on August 12, 1963, instituted a recruit training program in human relations.[65] He stressed that although this was a department effort, the individual officer plays the more significant part, for it is through a citizen's personal experience with a police officer that attitudes concerning the whole department are formulated.[66]

Still, one year later, rioting erupted in the Harlem community. As a result of the rioting, Acting-Mayor Screvane met with Harlem political groups to discuss the possible solution to the problems that underlay the rioting. On July 28, 1964, the acting mayor announced the assignment of more Black officers to the Harlem community. He also announced the planned reassignment of five white sergeants serving in Harlem to be replaced by five Black sergeants.[67]

Although this was a substantial change in the police department's policy toward Black and minority communities, it did not stem the rising hue and cry for more community participation in the selection of police officers who would serve in the community. Black political groups continued their pressure on the mayor, meeting with him and demanding that a Black commander be placed in charge of each of the precincts located in the predominantly Black Harlem community. They also demanded that the mayor have the police commissioner appoint immediately a Black inspector to head the police division covering the central Harlem area.[68]

On August 7, 1964, in response to the protest and demands of the Harlem community, the police commissioner assigned Capt. Lloyd Sealy to the 28th Precinct, where he was placed in charge and made its commanding officer. Captain Sealy thus became the first Black officer in the New York City Police Department ever to be in charge of a Harlem precinct.[69]

On June 19, 1965, the following year, Capt. Eldridge Waith was assigned to the 32nd Precinct as its commanding officer. Thus he too joined Captain Sealy in achieving history in the New York City Police Department. Captain Waith became the second Black officer to command a Harlem precinct. In addition, he became the first Black officer to command the 32nd Precinct. [70]

During the same year, only one month later, on July 3, 1965, Police Commissioner Broderick announced to the public that police officers were responsible for their actions. He warned them against bias and advised them to resign if they could not respect the rights of minority groups.[71] This was, by far, the strongest language that a police commissioner in the history of the New York City Police Department had ever used in describing the duties and responsibilities of police officers as public servants. As a result of the commissioner's statements on the matter of police-community contact situations, the Patrolmen's Benevolent Association responded rather negatively to the strongly worded statement. They did in fact arouse racial feelings among the members of the New York City Police Department by not supporting the commissioner's stand on racial justice and moreover discouraged the active participation of its membership in programs initiated by the department to bridge the gap between the police and the communities wherein minority groups resided.[72]

Many of the white police officers in the New York City Police Department viewed the change in police policy toward minorities as the granting of "special treatment" for them. This in fact led to the continued polarization of the department's Black and white officers. This problem was dealt with by the Guardians Association president William H. Johnson, Jr. On April 2, 1966, the following year, the Guardians expressed concern over the growing racial incidents between Black and white officers on the force. The president of the association, representing 1,350 members, stated that the fraternal societies on the force tended to splinter police officers along ethnic and national lines. He also went on to articulate the growing awareness by the Black membership of the department that this type of behavior restricted the communication between the police and the minority communities throughout the city. The police department's hierarchy did not publicly respond to this statement nor did they give the association an indication that there would be an investigation into the matter.[73]

It is highly important to note that the method of discrimination practiced by the New York City Police Department did not differ radically from its earlier history, or from that of the Brooklyn Police Department in the 1890s. Many prospective Black police officers, as candidates, were effectively prevented from joining the force. The methods employed by the department were varied. One of the techniques utilized was the rejection of Black candiates on the grounds of the age-old "heart murmur" excuse.[74] Another was the rejection of Black candidates on the basis of bad evaluations as the result of the screening process that was undertaken by the white police sergeants and police officers who were already members of the force.[75] The awareness of this problem spread throughout the Black communities in the city. As a result, the New York City Council of Elected Negro Democrats urged an inquiry into the department's "poor" record of selection, assignment, and promotion of minority group members within the department as well as those attempting to join the force.[76] This stand by the council was based upon the disclosure of information on the numerical representation of minority groups on the New York City Police Department, the New York City Housing Police and the New York City Transit Police. These figures were released to the *New York Times* in February, 1966. They showed that only 5 percent to 6 percent of the New York City Police Department's membership was Black and Hispanic, whereas the New York City housing and transit police departments had closer to 30 percent Black and Hispanic officers on their forces.[77]

The reaction of the police commissioner and the mayor to the inequitable conditions on the force was unusually swift. On March 17, 1966, Police Commissioner Leary appointed Assistant Chief Inspector Sealy and Deputy Commissioner Thomas, both

Black men, to review the qualifications of all of the rejected Black and Hispanic applicants to the force.[78] They were instructed to prevent rejections of applicants on the basis of bias on the part of the investigating officers who handled the character investigations of all potential police candidates. Thus, this two-man board had partial veto power over the selection process in the New York City Police Department.[79]

In response to the recommendations of numerous federal and local reports and the continuing demand by the Black and Hispanic population in the city, Police Commissioner Leary and Mayor Lindsay announced that the City of New York would begin a drive to recruit 1,000 Black and Hispanic candidates for the position of police officer. A new and innovative program was started with the help of the federal government which sponsored the program with a grant of 2.9 million dollars.[80] The original police cadet training program was inaugurated on May 9, 1966.[81]

The main purpose of the cadet training program was to prepare young men (underrepresented minority group members in the main) to qualify for positions as police officer and police trainee in the New York City Police Department. While the cadets were being trained, they received approximately $70 per week.[82]

For five cycles each lasting approximately one year, from 1966 to 1971 this program was rather successful. Nearly 400 men were appointed to the ranks of the New York City Police Department as police officers or as police trainees.[83]

Although the original purpose of the cadet program in 1966 was to train underprivileged young men exclusively for the New York City Police Department, due to the austerity program in effect during the early 1970s, a "job freeze" was instituted. The direction of the program then shifted to the task of preparing participants for all meaningful positions in the criminal justice system throughout the metropolitan area.[84]

On July 6, 1966, Commissioner Leary responded to the demands of Black communities and began to assign Black and Hispanic police officers to these communities. In addition, the commissioner assigned minority police officers to the recreational areas of the city that were frequented by minority groups, ostensibly to bridge the gap between the police department and the minority groups in the city,[85] for during this period the summer months saw rioting of Blacks and Hispanics throughout areas of the city.

On July 27, 1966, Lt. Charles Oscar Henry became the first Black supervisor ever assigned to the 75th Precinct in Brooklyn. The Black residents of the 75th Precinct had repeatedly requested a Black supervisor for their community, and Lieutenant Henry, who had worked as a sergeant in Harlem and then in Bedford-Stuyvesant, got the post. The East New York section of Brooklyn had seen days of rioting and prolonged alienation between the police department and the Black community;[86] thus, the transferring of Lieutenant Henry to the 75th Precinct was still another example of the influence that Blacks had developed in relationship to the appointment and assignment of Black officers in the New York City Police Department.

Two months later, on September 27, 1966, Commissioner Leary appointed Assistant Chief Inspector Sealy to the position of commanding officer of the Patrol Borough Brooklyn North area. This was the highest post that a Black officer in the New York City Police Department had ever held.[87] The appointment of Assistant Chief Inspector Sealy to this position was also related to the civil disorder and alienation of the Black residents in Brooklyn.

During the same month, Inspector Eldridge Waith was appointed to the position of commanding officer of the 6th Division, which covers the Central Harlem area.[88] This too was a visible effort aimed at reducing racial calm, for the Central Harlem area had also seen days of violence and civil disorder.

The following year, on July 22, two Black New York City Police Department inspectors, Inspector Hill and Assistant Chief Inspector Waith, attended a "Black Power" conference held in Newark, New Jersey. The purpose of attending the meeting, as explained by both men, was to develop possible new insights into the causes of Black protest and to offer their help in developing ways to stem the violence that had been occurring in the

Black areas of cities throughout the country.[89] This type of behavior, on the part of Black high-ranking officers in the department, was a clear change from the old image of the Black police officer. The image that the Black inspectors were getting away from was that of a "Tom."[90]

The growing awareness of the identity of the Black police officer with his community was manifested again on June 16, 1968, when many Black police officers, with special leave from the department issued by Mayor Lindsay, were permitted to attend the Poor People's Solidarity Day rally in Washington, D.C. Once there, the Black New York City police officers involved themselves in helping to patrol and assist the Solidarity Day organization in making the rally a success.[91]

The Black fraternal association, the Guardians, was basically responsible in pressuring the police commissioner and Mayor Lindsay into permitting Black police officers to attend the rally. Thus, their actions indicated a further commitment not only to the Black membership of the department but also to the Black citizenry of the city and of the nation.[92]

The New York City Police Department continued to witness historic changes in the assignment and promotion of Black officers on the force. The Kerner Commission report of 1968 called for greater minority representation in the police departments throughout the country. The commission also recommended changes in those policies regarding the advancement of Black police officers. These recommendations and the city of New York's reaction to them were exemplified by the substantial increase in the number of Black officers on the force as well as by the increase in the number of high-ranking Black officers on the force. By 1969, there were approximately 2,000 Black and Hispanic police officers on the force.[93] In addition to this, by June 28, 1969, Inspector Hill and Assistant Chief Inspectors Sealy and Waith had experienced the swiftest career advancements of any New York City police officers in the history of the department.[94]

As the result in the increase of Blacks and Hispanics on the New York City Police Department and the extremely rapid promotion of Black officers to some of the highest ranks within the

department, many white police officers began to actively participate in reactionary groups. These white police officers also
increased their harassment of Black and Hispanic communities
as well as those Black and Hispanic police officers on the force.[95]

In 1970, the Guardians Association challenged the city of
New York and its police department to halt the alleged "station
house brutality" inflicted against Black and Hispanic persons
taken into custody. The Guardians Association went on to
warn of a possible armed confrontation between Black and white
officers in the department. The association's president, Sergeant
Perry, disclosed in detail allegations the threats and harassment
of Black and Hispanic officers by white police officers on the
force. City officials and the police department brass declined to
respond to these allegations of misconduct on the part of some
of the white membership in the department.[96] Today William
Perry is deputy police commissioner, community affairs.

There were further consequences as a result of the statements
made by the Guardians Association, for Guardians were treading
on "sacred ground."[97] It was widely known by many of the city's
Blacks and Hispanics that on occasion some of them had in fact
been beaten up by New York City police officers. However, it is
one thing for the public to assert this belief and another for police
officers, who are members of the same police department, to
substantiate this belief by providing dates, times, and places of
these atrocities. This action on the part of the Guardians further
alienated the white and Black police officers in the department, for
it has long been a standard that a police officer should never "rat"
on another, regardless of the circumstances. This, therefore, was
a breach of the informal rules and regulations, which govern the
membership of the city's police force just as strongly as do the
formal rules and regulations. In fact the breaching of the "secrecy
norm" has in some cases caused severe emotional and physical
harm to officers that were "guilty" of this breach.[98]

As a result of the Guardians' action, Black police officers were
indiscriminately harassed by the white membership of the department. This harassment was subtle because it was through the
supervisory positions of authority that the white membership of

the department was able to effectively retaliate in dispensing assignments that were displeasing and in "closer supervision" of Black personnel, which resulted in Black officers' receiving more department complaints against them.[99]

The various forms of bias and discrimination by the New York City Police Department would continue for many of the Black officers on the force as well as those attempting to enter the department. The result would be a continued mistrust existing between the Black and white police officers in the department.

## NOTES

1. William B. Lockart, Yale Kamisar, Jesse H. Choper, *Constitutional Rights and Liberties* (New York: West Publishing Co., 1967), p. 815.
2. Ibid., p. 809.
3. Baker, *Following the Color Line,* p. 81.
4. Stokely Carmichael, Charles V. Hamilton, *Black Power* (New York: Random House, 1967), pp. 154-55.
5. Chambers, pp. 177-87.
6. H. R. Manhood, *Pressure Groups in American Politics* (New York: Charles Scribner's Sons, 1967), pp. 198-202.
7. Abe Fortas, *Concerning Dissent and Civil Disobedience* (New York: The New American Library, 1968), pp. 66-67.
8. Woodward, p. 174.
9. Ibid., pp. 141-42.
10. Hughes, et al., pp. 318-19.
11. V. O. Key, Jr., *Politics, Parties and Pressure Groups* (New York: Thomas Cromwell Publishers, 1964), p. 57.
12. U.S. Department of Commerce, Bureau of Census, *United States Census of Population:* 1960, vol. 2, *Characteristics of the Population,* pt. 5, New York.
13. *New York Amsterdam News,* 18 February 1956.
14. A. C. Ivy and Irvin Ross, *Religion and Race: Barriers to College?* (New York Public Affairs Committee, 1949, Pamphlet 153.

15. Michael Harrington, *The Other America* (New York: Penguin Books, 1964), pp. 64-66.
16. New York Harlem Youth Opportunities Unlimited, *Report on Youth in the Ghetto* (New York: 1964), pp. 166-80.
17. Clark, *Dark Ghetto,* pp. 27-28.
18. William Brink and Louis Harris, *Black and White* (New York: Simon & Schuster, 1967), p. 51.
19. Wormser, p. 441.
20. Eric C. Lincoln, "The Black Revolution in Cultural Perspectives," *Union Seminary Quarterly Review,* XXIII, 3 (Spring 1968): 35.
21. Thomas F. Pettigrew, "Racially Separate or Together," *Journal of Social Issues,* XXV, 1 (1969): 3-4.
22. Chambers, pp. 224-25.
23. James H. Cone, *Black Theology and Black Power* (New York: Seabury Press, 1969), pp. 12-14.
24. John Hope Franklin, *Color and Race* (Boston: Beacon Press, 1969), pp. 80, 81, 338, 339.
25. Brinks, Supplementary Statistical Tables, Appendix.
26. Fred I. Greenstein, *The American Party System and the American People* (Englewood Cliffs, N.J.: Prentice-Hall, Inc., 1963), pp. 99-101.
27. *New York Times,* June, July, August, 1963.
28. Many of the national broadcasting networks as well as the newspapers referred to the summer months as "the long hot summers."
29. Hughes, et al, pp. 338-39.
30. Ibid.
31. Handlin, *Race and Nationality,* pp. 136-37.
32. Otto Kerner, et al., "Report of the National Advisory Commission on Civil Disorders," 0291-729, U.S. Government Printing Office, 1968, pp. 1-14, 157-69, 219-21.
33. Ibid.
34. LEAP-Law Enforcement Assistance Program. Safe Streets Acts, Omnibus Crime Control Acts-Funding for various programs, "Affirmative Action" programs on the part of the federal, state, and local governments.

35. *New York Times,* 1 January 1953.
36. Ibid.
37. *New York Times,* 23 August 1951.
38. *New York Amsterdam News,* 7 May 1966.
39. *New York Times,* 1 January 1953.
40. *New York Times,* 16 December 1953.
41. Interview with Bracy.
42. Ibid.
43. "Prize Rookie," *Jet Magazine,* June 2, 1955, p. 59.
44. *New York Times,* 22 June 1956.
45. Anonymous interview, New York City Police Department, Personal Section, June, 1975.
46. Information obtained by surveying the U.S. Census Reports for the periods of 1940, 1950, and 1960 regarding Black graduates from high schools, two-year colleges, four-year colleges, and graduate schools.
47. Material obtained from a personal interview with Inspector Charles Henry, June 1975.
48. A "124-man" is a clerical assignment consisting of filing, typing, and other office duties.
49. Material obtained from a personal interview with Deputy Inspector Hamilton Robinson, July, 1975.
50. Material obtained from a personal interview with Deputy Inspector Glanvin Alveranga, July, 1975.
51. Material obtained from a personal interview with Captain Richard McBride, June, 1975.
52. Material obtained from a personal interview with Captain DeForest Taylor, June, 1975.
53. *New York Amsterdam News,* 18 February 1956.
54. *New York Amsterdam News,* 22 March 1958.
55. *New York Post,* 21 June 1959.
56. Interview with Bracy.
57. Interview with Mitchelson.
58. From 1964 to 1968, these areas of the city saw numerous racial disorders and protest (see New York newspapers).
59. *New York Times,* 13 July 1959.

60. *New York Amsterdam News,* July and August editions, 1959.

61. James Baldwin, "Fifth Avenue, Uptown," *Man Alone* (New York: Dell Publishing Co., 1962), pp. 352-53.

62. *New York Times,* 19 August 1959.

63. *New York Amsterdam News,* 19 August 1959.

64. George O'Connor and Charles G. Vanderbosch, *The Patrol Operation, Gaithersberg,* Md., International Association of Chiefs of Police, 1967, p. 10.

65. *New York Times,* 12 August 1963.

66. Ibid.

67. *New York Times,* 28 July 1964.

68. Ibid.

69. *New York Times,* 7 August 1964.

70. *New York Times,* 19 June 1965.

71. *New York Times,* 3 July 1965.

72. Information obtained through interviews with Black and white police officers who were working during this period on the New York City Police Department, January 1975-December 1976.

73. *New York Times,* 2 April 1966.

74. Interviews with New York City police officers.

75. "Ethnic Distribution and Retention Rate," PoliceAcademy Personnel Unit.

76. Interviews with New York City Police Officers.

77. *New York Times,* February and March, 1966.

78. *New York Times,* 17 March 1966.

79. Ibid.

80. *New York Times,* 9 May 1966.

81. Law Enforcement Cadet (Police) Training Program under "Manpower" Cycle 1, May 9, 1966, pp. 1-4.

82. *New York Times,* 9 May 1966.

83. "Manpower," pp. 2, 3.

84. Preparation for exams for the following positions: Parking Enforcement Agent; Federal Protective Officer; Correctional Officer (NYCDC); and Patrol Officer, Port of New York Authority.

85. *New York Times,* 6 July 1966.
86. *New York Times,* 27 July 1966.
87. *New York Times,* 27 September 1966.
88. *New York Times,* 30 September 1966.
89. *New York Times,* 22 July 1967.
90. Alex Poinsett, "The Dilemma of Black Policemen," *Ebony,* (May 1971): 126-27.
91. *New York Times,* 17 June 1968.
92. Information obtained through interviews with Black police officers who had at one time played an active role in the Guardians Association, May-September 1976.
93. *New York Times,* 30 June 1969.
94. *New York Times,* 28 July 1969.
95. *New York Times,* 16 June and 5, 6, 7, 8 September 1968.
96. *New York Times,* 21, 22 June 1970.
97. Niederhoffer, p. 186.
98. Ibid., pp. 192-94.
99. Personal interviews with Black and Hispanic members of the department.

# VI

## The Disruptive and Unfulfilled Years

From 1971 to 1977, the fifth generation of Blacks entered the New York City Police Department. Hence, there would be three generations of Blacks on the police force, the third, fourth, and fifth.

During these few years, Blacks representative of the third generation would advance to some of the highest ranking positions in the department. Simultaneously, the fourth generation would increase the number of Blacks holding midlevel supervisory ranks in the departments (sergeants and lieutenants). While the third and fourth generations of Blacks were achieving success, the fifth generation of Blacks was achieving a different kind of success. It would be the fifth generation of Blacks that would increase the total number of Blacks on the New York City Police Department by a substantial number. It would also be the highest number of Black women to the force since the first Black woman entered the department in 1917.[1]

Many of the changes that occurred in the New York City Police Department, however, were contingent upon the national and local events that would play a dominant role in creating changes in the social, political, and economic life of the American public. Some of these changes would wreak havoc on the dollar, on price and wage scales, and on governmental services both local and national.

In 1971, the State Investigations Commission began hearings into the alleged corruption in the New York City Police Department.[2] Later that same year, the Knapp Commission probed into similar charges involving members of the New York City Police

91

Department.³ By 1972, the Knapp Commission had concluded most of its initial investigation into alleged corruption in the department and had issued statements regarding it. However, the most impressive and consistent testimony came from a New York City police officer named Frank Serpico who had worked in the plainclothes units which were supposed to investigate and arrest wrongdoers involved in gambling and narcotics violations. Officer Serpico painted a picture of corruption that was massive, commonplace, and accepted as a way of life by too many New York City police officers regardless of rank.⁴

As the result of the Knapp Commission findings and recommendations, the citizens of New York City⁵ and the nation were once again confronted with governmental ineptness, attempted coverup, and lack of honesty and integrity on the part of public officials. The need for change in the department was dealt with by Police Commissioner Patrick Murphy. He embarked on new, innovative programs and policies aimed at cleaning up the department. The commissioner developed new internal investigative units and stationed them strategically at every precinct in the city.⁶ The entire department was put on notice that the police commissioner and the city of New York would not tolerate corruption of any kind by any member of the force.⁷ As a result of the continued exposure of the department to the public of its many weaknesses, the state government set up an office of special prosecutor to investigate the corruption in the department. Shortly thereafter, Maurice Nadjari was named to this position and almost immediately began to investigate and apprehend police officers involved in illegal activities.⁸ The news media covered many a story of how police officers assigned to the various vice squads were in fact being paid off *not* to make arrests, and to inform criminals of any known attempts by fellow officers or other agencies to investigate them.

As a result of the Knapp Commission hearings, the appointment of Special Prosecutor Nadjari, and numerous changes in the department by Commissioner Murphy, the police force suffered a lowering of morale. This situation was also compounded by the negative reactions of the public toward members of the New York City Police Department. Unfortunately, police officers who were not involved in corrupt activities also suffered.[9]

With the preceeding conditions as a backdrop, the fifth generation of Blacks entered the New York City Police Department. Many of these individuals entering the police academy wanted to change the image of the department.

During the period of January, 1973-October, 1974, 4,003 probationary police officers were appointed to the New York City Police Department, including the largest number of Blacks ever to enter the department. There were, in fact, 601 Blacks appointed to the force;[10] of this total, 448 were men, and 153, women. One of the most impressive statistics about these recruits, however, was their retention rate. Of the 448 Black men who entered the department, 407, or 90.85 percent were retained after completing the academy and assigned to field commands. Of the 153 Black women who entered the department, 137, or 89.54 percent were retained. This may be because of the average age of those Black police officers appointed in the department generally speaking, the older one is the more settled and mature one tends to be.

By November, 1974, there were 2,508 Blacks in the New York City Police Department. This figure represented more than there had been in the history of the department. Also besides the increase in the total number of Blacks on the force, there were more Blacks in supervisory capacities than there had ever been in its history. As of November, 1974, there were ninety-three Black sergeants, twenty-eight Black lieutenants, two Black captains, two Black deputy inspectors, three Black full inspectors, one Black deputy chief inspector, and one Black bureau chief.[11] This is important, for at no time in the department's history were there ever nine or more Blacks with the rank of captain or better on the force. It is additionally important for the reader to be aware that ranks above captain are based upon appointment and are not civil service positions, based upon examinations. In other words, there are seven Blacks on the force holding positions that are based upon appointment. This is not to imply that any of these officers, or any others for that matter, were not qualified for these positions.

The appointment to a position of deptuy inspector or higher is based upon a number of important factors, some of which are: intelligence, experience, originality, receptiveness, teaching ability, personality, knowledge of human behavior, courage, tenacity, a sense of justice and fair play, political support for the advancement generated by other members of the force, political support for the advancement generated by individuals or groups outside the department, morale, educational achievements, and integrity among others.[12] Since some of the previously mentioned factors have traditionally played a role in the selection process of officers appointed to high positions in the department, it should not be surprising to find that many of these factors had a bearing on those Black officers also selected and advanced to high positions. One of the most impressive factors about these officers is that *all* of them have attended college; five out of the nine hold bachelor's degrees, and two out of these five are presently completing their studies for master's degrees.[13]

Although the accomplishments of Blacks in the New York City Police Department seemed to be gathering momentum during the early years of the 1970s, the fiscal crunch that the city was experiencing detrimentally affected its services, and the department was not exempt from the shift in economic policies. The mayor and the city council set up an austerity budget for the city of New York. As matters became worse, the mayor announced further cutbacks in the city's vital services in the way of budget cuts that allowed for the functioning of the various city agencies, but at a bare minimum. The mayor also utilized the method of attrition to combat the economic crunch that the city was experiencing.[14] Although the various city agencies were not hiring new civil service employees, this alone was not adequate to aid the city in its fight to maintain economic integrity. As a result, the city of New York was moving near complete economic chaos. At this point, Mayor Beame took drastic measures to insure against bankruptcy, one being massive layoffs of civil service workers, including New York City Police Department personnel. On July 19, 1975, the mayor announced that the city would lay off 19,000 city employees; of this total figure, 5,000 were New York City police officers.[15] The Blacks and Hispanics, who had entered the department in substantial numbers during the early part of 1970, were most drastically affected by the layoffs. Of the 2488 Blacks on the job prior to the layoffs on July 19, 1975, 416 were laid off, bringing the total to only 2072 as of July 20, 1975.[16] The same condition held true for the Hispanic police officers. Prior to July 19, 1975, there were 1014 Hispanic officers on the job; 216 were laid off, leaving a total of 802 Hispanic officers on the force.[17]

This situation appeared to have eased when, on July 26, 1975, the mayor recalled approximately 2000 police officers back to the department.[18] However, though this was a sizable number of police officers coming back to the force the layoffs still disproportionately affected the Black, Hispanic, and female police officers in the department, the reason being that many of the Black and Hispanic police officers came into the department after 1969. Since civil service seniority determines who will be laid off and who will not, the Blacks, Hispanics, and women, who were the "last hired," were essentially the "first fired." To add to this problem, the mayor announced on October 14, 1975, that the city would have to lay off an additional 900 police officers before the end of the year.[19] Obviously, this would have further eliminated many of the Black, Hispanic, and female police officers who came into the New York City Police Department in the early 1970s had it been carried out.

Hence, the layoffs have been a tremendous setback for minorities in the city of New York. This holds true for many of the Black, Hispanic, and female police officers who were employed in the police department. Without the fifth generation of Black police officers on the force, the continued advancement of Black police officers in the New York City Police Department would come to a sudden halt.

Besides the dire effects that the city's layoffs had on the Black and Hispanic police officers, there were other factors which had an equally dire effect upon the growth and advancement potential of Blacks and Hispanics in the New York City Police Department. Although Black police officers had made tremendous gains in the department during the latter part of the 1960s, in the way of promotional advancements and assignments to command functions, the early 1970s appear to be the period in which these gains were reversed as the result of "fiscal policies." For example, the number of Black administrators has increased over what it was ten years ago; however, less than ten years ago there were two Black borough commanders, Assistant Chief Inspector Sealy in Brooklyn North and Assistant Chief Inspector Waith in Manhattan North. Both of these police officers commanded officers that were assigned to predominantly Black and Hispanic communities. Although these areas of the city experienced growth in their Black and Hispanic populations,[20] and the advancement of Black officers in the department had been very much contingent upon the political activities of various pressure groups in these communities as pointed out in chapter five, much of the clamor on the part of those Blacks and Hispanics seems to have died down. This is important for Black and Hispanic communities throughout the city. Since the retirement of Chief Mitchelson from the force in 1977 and the promotion of Bracy to assistant chief inspector, the latter is the highest ranking Black in the department.

This situation is further compounded by the actual "job-functions" that the other seven Black officers are assigned to. For, as the result of the restructuring of the department during the early part of 1973, the department did away with the command position of divisional commanders, replacing it with that of zone coordinator.[22] Hence, the level of development for potential borough commanders was removed by the department. This effectively removed a position that many of the older and higher ranking members of the department had to have experienced before being advanced to a higher rank. The zone coordinators are actually part of the borough commander's staff and carry out the functions of staff members. The divisional commanders had more flexibility in how they ran their divisions; therefore, it was not uncommon for these commanders to institute various policies according to the needs of their divisions. This decentralized form of administration was scrapped and a more centralized form replaced it. For the most part, it is at this particular point that Black administrators are missing out on the chance for greater input into the way the various precincts operate throughout the city, especially in those areas where there is a predominant Black and Hispanic population. For in the 1960s there were Black divisional commanders in Harlem, Bronx, Brooklyn, and Queens.

There appears to exist some evidence of complacency on the part of a number of Black and Hispanic police officers in the department. Many interviews with members of the department have shown this attitude on the part of many Black and Hispanic officers assigned to the various detective commands as "white-shield" detectives or as detectives with different grade status. Many of these officers expressed a satisfaction in their present assignments as detectives. They did not seem to care, one way or the other, about being promoted to a higher rank in the department. This attitude may have resulted from the fact that many of the Black and Hispanic police officers who acquire detective status have traditionally had to work harder for it than their white counterparts. Hence, detective status means more to them. The reader should also be aware that detective status is by appointment and not based on civil service competitive examinations, and that the officers assigned to this rank in the department can be reassigned to the status of police officer. Besides, the rank of detective pays more than the rank of police officer.

There presently exists a disproportionate amount of Black detectives in comparison to the amount of Black supervisors in the department, which has 394 Black detectives and 3583 white detectives. This means that Black detectives represent 10.9 percent of the total number of detectives in the New York City Police Department. On the other hand, there are 131 Black supervisors compared to 4190 white supervisors, including sergeants and superior ranks. Black supervisors represent 3.1 percent of the entire supervisory personnel in the department while they represent 10.9 percent of the total detective personnel. Hence, Blacks are overrepresented proportionately in the detective commands and assignments and underrepresented in the supervisory levels in the department.

The problem above is overshadowed only by the statistical information about Black female officers in the New York City Police Department. There are presently only 81 Black female police officers in the department, or .24 percent of the total number of female New York City police officers. The pattern for underrepresentation of Black females in the department is a historic one. However, it persists and is even more alarming when one examines the statistical information on the breakdown of Black female officers on supervisory levels. There is only *one* Black female supervisor in the entire New York City Police Department. If this isn't shocking enough, her rank is that of sergeant. In other words, there are no Black female police officers above the rank of sergeant. Its significance becomes clearer when one sees that this figure represents .04 percent of the number of sergeants in the department and only .00023 percent of the total number of supervisory personnel in the department. Therefore, unfortunately, Black females still continue to be affected by racial and sexual bias on the part of the New York City Police Department.

Thus, the third, fourth, and fifth generations of Black police officers and their respective families were shocked and dismayed by the fiscal plight of New York City that caused the laying off of numerous Black and Hispanic police officers. As if these events were not enough for Blacks and Hispanics to bear, other more tragic events unfolded during the 1970s. By comparison, the layoffs had a lesser effect upon Blacks and Hispanics than the deaths of Black police officers and Black youths as the result of actions taken by white police officers. Some of the root causes for these recent tragedies can be found in the social and political structure of the New York City Police Department. As was indicated in the preceding chapters, undoubtedly there has existed for a long period two systems of justice operating in the department, one for Black and Hispanic civilians and police officers, the other for white civilians and police officers.

During the 1970s, the actions of white police officers toward Blacks, regardless of whether they were police officers or civilians, have further alienated Blacks and Hispanics from their white counterparts on the force. The following paragraphs will illustrate what unfortunately can happen when an unequal and unfair system is allowed to continue and develop in such a powerful public service agency as a police department.

On April 3, 1972, a Black detective, after chasing a suspect and attempting to subdue him, was shot to death in the vestibule of a Queens shoe store by a uniformed white police officer who apparently mistook him for a criminal. The detective was William R. Capers, forty-one years old, a second-grade detective assigned to the 16th Division, Burglary-Larceny squad in Queens. Capers had been on the force for nineteen years. The police officer who shot Detective Capers was Robert Kenny of the Queens Traffic District. Detective Capers and his partner, Detective Raymond L. Freedley, Jr., were assigned to the Jamaica area because of numerous accounts of purse snatchings and other minor crimes. While on assignment, both detectives saw three men carrying shopping bags in a parking lot just across 164th Street from the shoe store. As the detectives approached and stopped them, one of the three broke and fled across the street, pursued by Detective Capers. Capers fired a warning shot into the air as he chased him. Then, as Capers caught up with him in the doorway of the shoe store, he brought Police Officer Kenny to the scene. Mr. Philip Reich, the manager of the store, said that he had seen the man identified as Detective Capers dressed in regular street clothes following another man into the foyer of his store. He said that the detective had been "holding a gun" on the other man, and the store owner went on to say that he just assumed that the man with the gun was a police officer.[23]

When Police Officer Kenny arrived on the scene and observed a Black man holding a gun on another man, he assumed a protective position and opened fire on Detective Capers. Thus ended Detective William R. Capers's life and career with the New York City Police Department. Capers had been a police officer for nineteen years and had been highly decorated by the department for meritorious actions.[24] The matter was investigated under Deputy Inspector Paul Glaser and written into the books as mistaken identity and Police Officer Kenny was found to be without fault.[25]

On Monday morning, March 5, 1973, Police Officer Irving E. Wright, a brother of Assemblyman Samuel D. Wright of Brooklyn, was shot and killed by two police officers on a Harlem Street. It all began when Officer Wright, a Black man, was chasing an armed man who had just held up an all-night grocery store where Wright had been moonlighting (working). Police Officer Wright, thirty-four years old, and the father of four children, was off duty and in plain clothes but carrying a .38 special pistol as authorized when he was shot to death on West 111th Street just east of 7th Avenue at 2.30 A.M.

A department spokesman indicated that two white police officers, Sether and McShane, while on patrol, had observed Wright running down the street. The two officers left their vehicle and approached Wright from behind. The spokesman indicated that the officers claimed that they ordered Wright to stop. However, he spun around and fired one shot at them. Both officers returned gunfire in the direction of the alleged assailant and emptied both of their guns.[26]

A number of issues sprang up as a result of the shooting death of a Black police officer by two white officers. The entire matter was investigated by a grand jury. Part of the information the jury received was from the medical examiner's office. Dr. Frank B. Presswolla examined Wright's body. He concluded that Wright had been hit by six bullets, all of which entered the officer's sides. Dr. Presswolla went on to state that the angle of entry of the bullets into Wright's body indicated they had been fired a little from the rear. This obviously conflicted with the statements by Officers McShane and Sether, who had indicated that Officer Wright had turned toward them and had fired at them. For if, in fact, they had returned fire at that point, the question remains why the bullets did not enter Wright's body through the front instead of the sides, as indicated by Dr. Presswolla.[27]

On Friday, March 9, 1973, Sgt. Howard Sheffey, president of the Guardians Association, stated, "White policemen are shooting at Black people too damned fast. It is very strange," Sergeant

Sheffey said, speaking at the Guardian headquarters, "that tragic mistakes seem to happen to only Black police officers."

The presiding minister at Irving Wright's funeral was Rev. Gardiner Taylor at the Concord Baptist Church of Christ, at 883 March Avenue in Brooklyn. While Mr. Taylor was addressing the mourners, he stated, "It compels me to say that the trigger finger is likely to be more nervous in the kind of community where Irving Wright was killed. When the face is Black, the finger is likely to be just ever so slightly reluctant [not to shoot]."[28]

On the following day, March 10, 1973, the New York City Police Department reported that a packet containing an eighth of an ounce of cocaine might have been found on the body of Officer Irving Wright after he was fatally shot by the two white police officers. Assistant Chief Inspector Donald F. Cawley, in announcing the results of what he called "a thorough investigation," said that there were no suspicious circumstances in the shooting and that Officer Wright was not in criminal possession of the illegal drugs. The packet, reportedly found by a hospital attendant, had passed through several hands before the police took formal possession of it.[29]

Although a Manhattan grand jury convened to examine the information and circumstances involved in the shooting death of Officer Wright, they refused to return criminal charges against Officers McShane and Sether; in addition, no departmental trials were ever initiated by the New York City Police Department against either of the officers.

On June 7, 1973, a Black detective, William B. Jakes, of the Brooklyn Major Cases Unit was shot once in the abdomen. Jakes underwent surgery at Brookdale Hospital Medical Center, where he was listed in satisfactory condition. According to the police, there had been a stake-out of twenty to twenty-five men from the F.B.I., the N.Y.C.P.D. and the Queens district attorney's office. The men were positioned in the area of East New York around New Lots Avenue and Vermont Street. They were there in response to a vague tip that weapons were to be delivered to Black militants.[30] In the stake-out, Detective Jakes and his two partners, Officer Fred Lambert and Officer Rodney Hunt, were posted with shotguns on the roof of 440 New Lots Avenue, a three-story apartment building. At 10:15 A.M., an anonymous caller reported to the police that an intruder was on the roof. Two uniformed white police officers from the 75th Precinct, Andrew Scibelli and Louis Calcones, responded to the call in an RMP (radio motor patrol) and, in what a police spokesman said was an apparent communications breakdown or human error, "they were unaware of the stake-out."

At the top of the stairs, just below the roof, according to Deputy Police Commissioner Richard Kellerman, "They saw the door partly opened, they pushed the door and saw a shotgun." He went on, "The door started to close." Officer Calcones fired three shots, apparently through the open door since the door itself showed no holes in it. As a result of his actions, Detective Jakes was hit once in the abdomen. The detectives on the roof somehow realized the men below were fellow police officers because they did not return the fire, and Officer Lambert threw his shield through the door for identification and Officer Scibelli threw his police hat up the roof in response.[31] Another investigation was conducted by the New York City Police Department, but with negative results. Officer Calcones was vindicated from any wrongdoing.

A few months later, on December 14, 1973, just before Christmas, Detective Harold Maxwell, a white police officer, and John White, a Black police officer, both in plain clothes and unknown to each other, were chasing the same car thief, who allegedly had stolen a Cadillac. Officer White caught the suspect and placed him against the side of the car and began to frisk him. Thereupon, Officer Maxwell came upon the scene. He saw a "Black man" holding a gun on a "white man" and "naturally" assumed that Officer White was the suspect he had been chasing. Maxwell took cover behind a car and without warning began shooting at Officer White. Officer White was hit in the back of his right arm; he dropped his gun and ran wildly into the street to get out of the line of fire, but he still didn't see anyone. He started shouting, "I'm on the job," which is what cops use to identify themselves, but it didn't do any good. Officer White was shot again in the neck by Detective Maxwell. While White lay bleeding on the asphalt, Maxwell walked over and frisked him. He found Officer White's police shield, and only then did Detective Maxwell realize that he had shot a fellow officer.[32]

This shooting was the last straw for the Guardians Association. Sgt. Howard Sheffey spoke out against the incident when he stated, "We have eight incidents in recent years where Black policemen were shot by a white policeman. There is not one incident of a Black officer shooting a white officer." According to Sheffey and numerous other Black officers, they had held the belief for a long time that Blacks in the department were getting mowed down by their "brother" officers in blue an unusual number of times. The Guardians Association publicly threatened to call all Black plainclothes officers off their respective assignments unless there was some decisive action on the part of the police commissioner to correct the situation.[33]

As a result of these incidents, the New York City Police Department undertook a dramatic and innovative approach toward the curtailment of such tragedies. During the early spring of 1974, a new method for stopping alleged suspects by police officers in the field was presented in the in-service training program and the outdoor training program (shooting range) and continued on a daily basis in the roll-call training that officers receive prior to carrying out their assignments for each tour. The new feature dealt with the standardization of word usage that police officers would use in the field when ordering a suspect to stop. It was simple but to the point. "Police. Stop. Don't move." In addition to training members of the department to utilize the same words, the training also focused upon new techniques that were to be employed by a police officer upon approaching a possibly armed suspect.[34] Police officers were instructed to immediately size up the situation and to place themselves behind an object or structure that could afford them some real physical protection. Hence, it was believed that the officer approaching a suspect would have the following advantages:

1. He would protect himself from possibly being shot in a vital area of his body.
2. He would have a psychological advantage of temporary security, which might give him time to think more clearly and present less need to fire his weapon as quickly as he might, without the cover.
3. He might allow the suspect the ability to identify himself and not shoot him while he did so.

Police officers were also instructed that if one is off duty or on duty but in civilian clothes and is approached by uniformed police officers he is to do the following:

1. When ordered to stop, he is to cease all physical activity.
2. He is not to make sudden or any jerky movements.
3. He is to clearly state that he is a police officer, with his rank and name and possibly the unit he is assigned to.
4. In order to prevent the possibility of a plainclothes officer's being shot by a suspect accomplice after he has complied with the order to stop and/or to drop his weapon, the built-in safeguard to be used by the plainclothes officer is to ask about certain commonly used police clerical forms and/or jargon which is limited to police officers.[35]

Since the inception of this training program, no Black or Hispanic officer has been shot by a white police officer.

While the Black communities were already distraught and angered by the shootings of Black police officers by white police officers, another more serious problem emerged. Unarmed Black youths were being shot to death by white police officers. Clifford Glover, Claude Reese, Jr., Randolph Evans, and a Brooklyn College student, John Brabham, were all fatally shot by white police officers.

At about 5 A.M. in the morning of April 28, 1973, Thomas J. Shea, a white police officer, shot and killed Clifford Glover, a ten-year-old Black youth. According to Officer Shea and his partner, Officer Scott, the youth was shot while fleeing from them.

Police officer Shea was subsequently indicted for murder and became the first New York City police officer to be charged with murder for actions taken during the course of his duty. The P.B.A. provided legal funds, attorneys, and moral support for Shea. Rumors were circulated through the P.B.A. and the police department that Officer Shea and his partner were not getting a fair deal. The rumors further implied that both officers were being railroaded by the hierarchy in order to appease the Black community.[37]

Prior to and during the trial it was stated by Officer Shea that Clifford Glover had pulled a gun on him. However, according to Assistant District Attorney Albert Gaudelli, Officer Shea's actions indicated a depraved indifference to human life. He further stated that although Shea had indicated there had been a gun in the hands of the youth, no gun had ever been found. The district attorney's office had made frequent checks to the lot located in the Jamaica section of Queens where the youth was fatally shot. Moreover, according to the assistant district attorney, Clifford Glover had been accompanying his stepfather to work at 5 A.M. in the morning when Officers Shea and Scott, who were both in plainclothes and in an unmarked car, pulled up alongside the two on New York Boulevard near 112th Street. The officers had been looking for two male suspects wanted in connection with a taxi robbery. Officer Shea leaped from the car and shouted, "Halt, you Black-son-of-a-bitch," whereupon the man and the boy fled into a lot, where Officer Shea shot the youth in the back. As the two officers stood over the youth, one of them looked down at the bleeding youth and scowled, "Die you little fuck," words he thought would never be heard, but, unknown to the officer, were broadcast over a walkie-talkie that he carried.

While this was occurring, the stepfather kept running and stopped a passing patrol car. He told the officers that his boy had been shot. The policemen returned to the lot with the stepfather and took the youth to the hospital where he died. Officer Shea further alleged that the youth, after being shot and falling, gave the gun to the stepfather.

After a brief trial, eleven white men and one Black woman

acquitted Shea of murder. This verdict reaffirmed a policy that when it came to white police officer's shooting and killing Blacks, the possibility of these officers' being treated the same as ordinary citizens would not exist. Besides what Shea had done to little Clifford Glover, who was ten years old and weighed ninety pounds, Officer Shea had a history of violence, for this was his third incident in less than one year. At the time he shot Clifford Glover he was still facing charges of having pistol-whipped a fourteen-year-old boy, and had been accused of shooting an unarmed man in the neck.[38]

Officer Shea was later given a departmental trial and found guilty of conduct unbecoming an officer and related charges. He was subsequently dismissed from the force.

In June of 1974, Police Officer William L. Walker, white, was indicted by a Brooklyn grand jury for the shooting death of a young Black college student, John Brabham, whom the officer had reportedly stopped during a routine auto inspection. The officer claimed that he had been threatened with a toy gun that was later recovered from the scene of the incident. However, through an investigation by the police department and the district attorney's office, it was later established that Officer Walker had been seen with the same toy gun by his white fellow officers the evening before the incident, on April 9, 1973. It was also determined that the dead student was unarmed at the time of the incident.[39] Officer Walker was found not guilty after a short trial in New York Supreme Court in February of 1977.

Later that month, on June 24, 1974, a press release was issued from the police commissioner's office indicating that he was weighing a proposal to obtain wide psychological services for the department. Dr. Harvey Schlossberg was made director of psychological services. Although the services dealt with family problems, job-related problems, and understanding ways to deal with hostage situations (special negotiating teams) by the officers on the force, they failed to deal with the shooting of Black officers and unarmed Black civilians by white officers.[40]

On September 15, 1974, Claude Reese, Jr., a fourte-year-old Black youth was shot to death by a white police officer. The incident occurred in the evening as Reese and other Black youths were cleaning the basement of a building for the purpose of giving a party for one of their friends. Unknown to the youths, Officer Frank Bosco was responding to a burglary run at the same location. When he entered the premises the lighting was quite poor and the officer was unable to see very clearly. When the youths saw two white men entering the basement with guns drawn they began running. Officer Bosco shot and killed Claude Reese, who allegedly turned and pointed something at him. No weapon was ever found in the subsequent searches of the building. The shooting touched off two nights of racial disturbances in the Brownsville section of Brooklyn. Later that week five hundred people marched at City Hall in protest of the Claude Reese killing. Officer Bosco was stripped of his weapon and assigned to clerical duties outside the district that he worked in. A grand jury convened and investigated the matter. They held that the shooting death was an unfortunate and tragic, but unintentional, error since Officer Bosco believed his life was in imminent danger at the time and place of occurrence. Bosco was eventually terminated from the police department with a full medical disability as a result of the incident.[41]

On Thursday, November 25, 1976, Randolph Evans, a fifteen-year-old Black youth, was shot to death by Robert H. Torsney, a white policeman. Young Evans was killed shortly after Officer Torsney and five other policemen responded to an unfounded report of a man with a gun at 515 Fountain Avenue in the Cypress Hills Housing Project in the East New York section of Brooklyn. Upon leaving the building, Officer Torsney confronted Randolph Evans. Words were exchanged, at which time Torsney drew his revolver and fired one shot point blank into the head of young Evans. The youth was rushed to the hospital. Chief Mitchelson, a Black officer who is in charge of all uniform officers in the New York City Police Department, responded to the 75th Precinct. The Brooklyn district attorney's office also responded to the precinct and the shooting scene. The parents of the dead youth, numerous civilians, and police officers were interviewed by police department and the district attorney's office. Shortly thereafter a Brooklyn grand jury convened to examine all of the evidence in the case.[42]

On December 1, 1976, Officer Torsney was indicted on a charge of murdering Randolph Evans. He was the third police officer (all of whom were white) in three years to be indicted in the slaying of a Black youth. One officer, Thomas Shea, had been acquitted but later dismissed from the police department; another, William L. Walker, was acquitted last February by an all white jury. With regard to the actions of Officer Torsney, Cornelius J. Behan, chief of personnel for the New York City Police Department, stated, "We have a good system and it's working." Since the shooting incident he said, "Officer Torsney's records have been carefully examined and his fellow officers interviewed about his behavior. His files showed no citations, no reports of misconduct and that he never fired his gun on duty." He went on to say, "It was absolutely zero as to warning signs. He was one of the most average men we've ever come across." Douglas Weaving, P.B.A. president stated, "Torsney had to defend himself in a high crime area."[43]

After Officer Torsney was arrested, he was arraigned on charges of second-degree murder. He was represented by Edward M. Rappaport, a P.B.A. lawyer. He was a first held without bail, but another judge set his bail at $40,000. The money for bail was given by the P.B.A.

As a result of some of the statements made by the P.B.A.'s president as well as Rappaport, the Guardians Association voted unanimously to withdraw from the P.B.A. Sergeant Sheffey, president of the Guardians Association, noted that the P.B.A. had previously bailed out another white officer who had killed a Black youth. He went on to say, "The only time the P.B.A. bails out police officers is when the child killed is Black."[44] On November 30, 1977, Officer Torsney was acquitted of slaying Randolph Evans.[45]

It is important for the reader to be aware of a *New York Times* survey which showed that three out of every five persons killed by New York City police officers over the last few years were Black. This proportion is three times higher than Black representation in the city's population. Obviously, there is considerable merit to the Guardians Association's assertion that the reaction of the P.B.A. and the New York City Police Department to the investigation, indictment, trial and/or conviction of white police officers for shooting or beating to death Blacks and Hispanics is highly questionable.

Although most police officers felt that no white police officer would ever be found guilty of homicide, this feeling was changed on Saturday, November 5, 1977.[46] History was made that day when a white police officer, Thomas Ryan, was convicted by an all white jury of criminally negligent homicide in the beating death of a Hispanic suspect, Israel Rodriguez. The beating had occurred at the scene of an initial arrest and at the precinct stationhouse. The guilty verdict marked the first time that any on-duty police officer was convicted of slaying a suspect.

During the trial testimony, it was revealed that the unwritten "code of silence," which forbids officers from speaking out against fellow officers, was broken. Several officers, including Sgt. Richard Riccio, indicated in testimony that it was a common practice for police officers to lie in order to protect each other. Hence, one cannot but wonder how truthful and accurate was testimony given by police officers involved in the trials of fellow officers accused of illegally terminating the life of a suspect.

In addition to the foregoing, there have been incidents, during the 1970s, involving both white and Black police officers that are anything but normal. The overwhelming number of them have not reached the news media. Some of these incidents involve white officers' attempting to summons off-duty Black police officers' private cars, or attempting to arrest them, for no apparent reason. Other incidents involve Black and white officers, while on duty, engaged in fistfights. Still others involve white and Black officers, while on duty, drawing their weapons and pointing them at each other. So far this type of incident has resulted in what has been termed "a Mexican standoff."

Obviously, the present situation warrants immediate intervention on the part of the hierarchy in the police department. To wait and allow the situation to get further out of hand would be foolish and quite unwise. The police department must take a firm stand against any form of racial discrimination or bias on the part of any of its personnel. To fail to do so would be a breach of public trust and confidence in the police department.

The future isn't written yet. It is hoped that the conditions under which minorities work will rapidly be improved. However, much of the impetus for change will come from outside the police department, since the department has historically been entwined in a system of discrimination.

## NOTES

1. *The Negro Yearbook,* 1917, 1918, p. 53.
2. New York newspapers, April-August, 1971.
3. *New York Times,* January 9 and 20, February 25 and 26 1972.
4. Peter Maas, *Frank Serpico* (New York: Viking Publishing Co., 1973), p. 84.
5. *New York Times,* 8 January; 24, 28 March; 15 December 1972.
6. *New York Times,* 2 January 1972.
7. *New York Times,* 17 May 1972.
8. *New York Times,* 20, 28 September 1972.
9. New York City newspaper editorials, and comments by letters and statements to the press.
10. "Breakdown of Blacks in the New York City Police Department," Police Academy Personnel Unit.
11. New York City Police Department, Personnel Unit.
12. V. A. Leonard and Harry W. More, *Police Organization and Management* (New York: Foundation Press, 1971), p. 45.

13. Material obtained from interviews with the top-ranking Black police officers in the New York City Police Department, August, 1975.
14. Steven R. Weisman, *How New York Became a Fiscal Junkie, New York Times* magazine section, 17 August 1975, pp. 8, 9, 71-77.
15. *New York Daily News,* 19 July 1975.
16. New York City Police Department, Equal Opportunity Unit.
17. Ibid.
18. *New York Times,* 26 July 1975.
19. *New York Times,* 14 October 1975.
20. Maps of racial patterns in Brooklyn and Manhattan, U.S. Census, 1970.
21. *New York Times,* 8 March 1975.
22. Material obtained from personal interviews with past and present members of the New York City Police Department. In addition, material from New York City Police Department "In-Service Training" lectures, department memos, and the like.
23. *New York Times,* 3 April 1972.
24. *New York Amsterdam News,* 3 April 1972.
25. *New York Times,* 4 April 1972.
26. *New York Times,* 6 March 1973.
27. Ibid.
28. *New York Times,* 10 March 1973.
29. Ibid.
30. *New York Times,* 8 June 1973.
31. Ibid.
32. *New York Times,* 15 December 1973.
33. *New York Amsterdam News,* 15 December 1973.
34. New York City Police Department training units: Brooklyn North Area Unit Training, Firearms Unit Training City Island.
35. Ibid.
36. *New York Times,* 28 April 1973, 18 May 1974.
37. *New York Times,* 18 May 1974.

38. *New York Times*, 24 June 1974.
39. *New York Times*, 24 June 1974
40. *New York Times*, 16 September 1974.
41. *New York Times*, 26 November 1976.
42. *New York Times*, 1 December 1976.
43. *New York Amsterdam News*, 11 December 1976.
44. *New York Amsterdam News*, 11 December 1976.
45. *New York Times*, 30 November 1977.
46. *New York Times*, 6 November 1977.

# VII

## *Conclusion*

From 1890 to 1977, five generations of Black men and women have served the city of New York as police officers. Although in some cases considerable time has separated the generations of Black police officers, the patterns of racial bias and discrimination have remained constant. From the early beginnings to the present, Blacks have had to endure numerous emotional and physical hardships in order to pursue careers as police officers in the New York City Police Department. Even the preliminary examination, whether written or physical, has traditionally been subjected to a kind of arbitrariness on the part of the police department. Many of the younger Black officers who have entered the force in recent years indicated in interviews that they, like their predecessors, felt they must be examined by private, reputable physicians prior to submitting to an examination by a police surgeon to insure objectivity.

Although the number of Blacks in the police department had been increasing over the years, this pattern has changed and their number has diminished substantially recently. In November, 1974, there were 2,508 Black officers on the force. At the present time (November, 1977), there are approximately 765 male Hispanics, 1,728 male Blacks, and 430 female officers on the New York City Police Department. Collectively these minority groups make up 2,923, or 11 percent of a force which numbers 24,877. These figures are more alarming when they are further broken down. There are 765 male Hispanic officers and only 3 female Hispanic officers on the force. While the male Hispanic police officers are represented throughout the department in terms of rank—detectives, sergeants, lieutenants, and captain—the

113

female Hispanic police officers are represented only in the following ranks: 2 female Hispanic police officers and 1 female Hispanic detective. Although there are more Black police officers on the force (1,809), they still represent only 7 percent of the force. This includes the ranks of 1st-, 2nd-, and 3rd-grade detectives, police officers, 76 Black sergeants, 18 Black lieutenants, and 8 Black police officers with the rank of captain or above. While Black males represent .069 of the entire force, Black females represent only .003 of the total force. However in terms of their representation compared to the total number of white females on the force, they represent 19 percent of the total number, or 81 female officers on the force. Upon further examination of Black female officers on the force today, one finds that there is only one Black female sergeant and that is Sgt. Majorie Lewis, a twenty-six-year veteran, assigned to the Civilian Complaint Review Board. There are no higher ranking Black female officers than Sergeant Lewis and there are no Hispanic female officers with supervisory rank on the force at all.

Since Sgt. Majorie Lewis is eligible to retire from the force, one wonders when and who will take her place in this rank, or possibly advance to even higher ranks in the department. Although age is a factor in the case of Lewis, there have been other factors which have contributed to the general decline of Black males and females and Hispanic males and females on the force. They are as follows: (1) layoffs, (2) attrition, (3) resignation, (4) retirement, (5) dismissal, (6) disability, and (7) death. All of these factors have eroded the potential gains that the fifth generation of Black officers could have made.

Moreover, time is working against the continued advancement of Blacks on the force. All of the high-ranking Black police officers have completed their twentieth year of service; therefore, they are eligible for retirement. In fact, the average length of service for the eight top-ranking Black officers in the department is 24.62 years. All can retire today. Once these officers retire, who will take their places? How long will it take before a younger officer can fill the slots? As of the present time, there are only two Black lieutenants on the job who have been placed on the captain's list. This by no means assures that they will be advanced in rank. As a matter of fact, the city of New York has instituted measures that have effectively limited the normal promotions for civil service personnel in the department. Since it took several years for the top-ranking Black officers to acquire their present positions, it will be some time before younger Black officers replace them.

If the city continues to experience economic hardship and becomes unable to sufficiently bail itself out, it seems very doubtful that all of the remaining laid-off New York City police officers (1700) will be rehired. Hence, it may be some time before members of the fifth generation of Black officers will be given the chance to achieve advancement within the department.

As this study shows, it is quite evident that racial discrimination and sexual bias, unfortunately, are significant factors in determining the outcome of various situations in the New York City Police Department. Since it seems historically to be the case that the department cannot, in and of itself, correct its own discriminatory practices against minority personnel and civilians, it is evident that the situation warrants the introduction of an outside agency.

It is recommended that:

1. Such an agency be from the federal sector, rather than the city or state, and be empowered to investigate allegations of racial discrimination and sexual bias on the part of the New York City Police Department toward Blacks, Hispanics, and women in the department.
2. The agency, after a careful investigation into alleged discriminatory acts, should clearly establish whether or not the New York City Police Department has engaged and/or still is engaged in such illegal practices.
3. The agency should have the power not only to recommend changes, but also to insure that its recommendations are carried out with deliberate speed.

Some of the programs that such an agency would have to institute in order to facilitate constructive changes in the department are as follows:

1. A program for the recruitment, hiring, training, and placement of Blacks, Hispanics, and women as police officers in the New York City Police Department. This program should also include the reevaluation and possible upgrading in position, assignment, and/or rank of all minority police officers, especially when bias and discrimination have been intentionally used against minority members of the service.
2. A medical program for the annual testing and examination of all members of the service in order to determine if they are in fact psychologically and physically fit for duty. In addition, it should be determined if each member of the service should be allowed to continue to carry or possess a firearm.
3. A program for the development and utilization of new criteria and methods for the observation, reporting, and evaluation of all members of the service. This program should include, as a supervisory responsibility, evaluation to determine whether or not a police officer, regardless of rank, uses unreasonable and unwarranted physical force and/or verbal abuse against members of the service as well as against civilians.

Unfortunately, a number of police officers will reject one or more of the aforementioned recommendations or special programs. The basis for this possible rejection may be found in the working attitude of many white police officers who feel that being a police officer is a privilege due only them (as an ethnic group). Hence, the introduction of almost "anything new" in the police department is viewed by the rank and file with a great deal of skepticism. This is especially true when "anything new" includes a Black, Hispanic, or woman's face. Likewise, this attitude prevails toward changes in the "traditional procedure" used in the department.

Nevertheless, the above recommendations and special programs will benefit, in the short and long run, all members of the force. The advantages of instituting the medical program, alone, are enormous. An annual physical and psychological examination of all police officers on the force could prove to be one of the most innovative concepts in law enforcement today. Such a program could detect heart trouble, glaucoma, diabetes, cancer, and other diseases, illnesses, injuries, and general medical problems that people may not be aware of. One of the most important aspects of medicine today is early detection of ailments and the practice of preventive medicine. Surely, a member of the service, regardless of his or her sex, race, color, creed, nationality, etc., would appreciate the detection of a medical problem before the condition got worse or caused injury to himself or to others. Thus, such a program would also be beneficial to families of police officers.

Although Blacks, Hispanics, and women compose a significant percentage of the total population in the city of New York, they are underrepresented in the New York City Police Department. Since these same Blacks, Hispanics, and women pay federal, state and local taxes, and since it is quite illegal for any governmental agency to discriminate against any person on the basis of sex, race, religious creed or belief, or nationality, the funding of the New York City Police Department is legally on shaky grounds. If the New York City Police Department does not develop a comprehensive program for the upgrading of its Black, Hispanic, and female officers as well as adequate recruitment and hiring programs, federal funding of the New York City Police Department may be withheld.

# Bibliography

Alex, Nicholas. *Black in Blue*. New York: Appleton-Century Crofts, 1969.

Astor, Gerald. *The New York Cops*. New York: Charles Sribner's Sons, 1971.

Baker, Roy Standard. *Following the Color Line*. New York: Harper & Row Publishers, 1964.

Baldwin, James. "Fifth Avenue, Uptown." *Man Alone*, pp. 352-53. Edited by Eric and Mary Josephson. New York: Dell Publishing Co., Inc., 1962.

Barron, Milton L. *American Minorities*. New York: Alfred A. Knopf Company, 1962.

Blumberg, Abraham S. *Criminal Justice*. New York: Quadrangle Books, 1970.

Brink, William and Harris, Louis. *Black and White*. New York: Simon & Schuster, 1967.

*Brooklyn Daily Eagle,* 8 March 1891-14 December 1900 .

Brooklyn North Area Unit Training (Handout). New York City Police Department, 1974.

Carmichael, Stokely and Hamilton, Charles V. *Black Power*. New York: Random House, 1967.

Chambers, Bradford. *Chronicles of Black Protest*. New York: New American Library, 1968.

*Chicago Defender,* 9 July 1955.

Clark, Kenneth B. *Dark Ghetto*. New York: Harper & Row Publishers, 1965.

Cone, James H. *Black Theology and Black Power*. New York: Seabury Press, 1969.

Da Silva, Benjamin, Finkelstein, Milton, Loshin, Arlene. *The Afro-American in United States History.* New York: Globe Book Company, 1969.

Equal Opportunity Unit (Handouts). New York City Police Department.

Firearms Training Unit (Handout), City Island. New York City Police Department.

Franklin, John Hope. *Color and Race.* Boston: Beacon Press, 1969.

Fortas, Abe. *Concerning Dissent and Civil Disobedience.* New York: The New American Library, 1968.

Greenstein, Fred I. *The American Party System and the American People.* Englewood Cliffs, N.J.: Prentice-Hall, Inc., 1963.

Handlin, Oscar. *The Newcomers.* New York: Doubleday & Co., Inc., 1962.

_____. *Race and Nationality in American Life.* New York: Doubleday & Co., Inc., 1950.

Harrington, Michael. *The Other America.* New York: Penguin Books, 1964.

Honigman, John J. *Personality in Culture.* New York: Harper & Row Publishers, 1967.

Hughes, Langston, Lincoln, Eric, Meltzer, Milton. *The Pictorial History of Black Americans.* New York: Crown Publishers, 1968.

Huthmacher, Joseph J. *A Nation of Newcomers.* New York: Dell Publishing Co., Inc., 1967.

In-Service Training Lectures (Handouts). New York City Police Department.

Ivy, A. C. and Ross, Irvin. *Religion and Race: Barriers to College?* New York: New York Public Affairs Committee, 1949, Pamphlet, p. 153.

Kerner, Otto, et al. *Report of the National Advisory Commission on Civil Disorders.* U.S. Government Printing Office: 0291-729, 1968.

Key Jr., V. O. *Politics, Parties and Pressure Groups.* New York: Thomas Cromwell Publishers, 1964.

Law Enforcement Cadet (Police) Training Program under "Manpower," Cycle 1, May 9, 1966, pp. 1-4.

Leonard, V. A. and More, Harry W. *Police Organization and Management.* New York: Foundation Press, 1971.

Lincoln, Eric. "The Black Revolution in Cultural Perspectives." *Union Seminary Quarterly Review* xxiii, 3 (Spring 1968): 35.

Lockart, William B., Kamisar, Yale, and Choper, Jesse H. *Constitutional Rights and Liberties.* St. Paul, Minn.: West Publishing Company, 1967.

Louell, Jr., John. "Youth Programs of Negro Improvement Groups." *Journal of Negro Education* 3 (July 1940): 381.

McDonagh, Edward C. and Simpson, Jon E. *Social Problems: Persistent Challenges.* New York: Holt, Rinehart & Winston, Inc., 1965.

Maas, Peter. *Serpico.* New York: Viking Publishing Company, 1973.

Manhood, H. R. *Pressure Groups in American Politics.* New York: Charles Scribner's Sons, 1967.

Mather, Frank Lincoln, ed. *Who's Who of the Colored Race.* Chicago: Memento Edition, 1915.

N.A.A.C.P. "Letter to President Roosevelt." *Crises,* Vol. 48 (1941): 71, 72, 81, 83, 85.

*New York Age,* 12 January 1935.

*New York Amsterdam News,* January Editions 1946-11 December 1976.

*New York Daily News,* 7 December 1941-19 July 1975.

New York Harlem Youth Opportunities Unlimited. *Report on Youth in the Ghetto.* New York: Haryou, 1964.

"News in Review." *Jet Magazine* May, 1954, p. 10.

*New York Post,* 28 June 1938-24 November 1965.

*New York Sun,* 7 January 1934.

*New York Times,* 28 June 1911-30 November 1977.

*New York Tribune,* 17 July 1931, 7 January 1935.

*New York World,* 22 May 1926.

Niederhoffer, Arthur. *Behind the Shield: The Police in Urban Society.* New York: Doubleday & Co., 1967.

O'Conner, George and Vanderbosch, Charles G. *The Patrol Operation.* Gaithersberg, Md.: International Association of Chiefs of Police, 1967, p. 10.

Ogburn, William F. and Nimkoff, Meyer F. *Sociology.* Boston: Houghton-Mifflin, 1968.

Personnel Unit (Handout). New York City Police Department.

Pettigrew, Thomas F. "Racially Separate or Together." *Journal of Social Issues.* xxv, 1 (1969): 3-4.

Peyton Jr., Thomas Roy. *A Quest for Dignity, Autobiography of a Negro Doctor.* Los Angeles: Warren F. Lewis, 1950.

Poinsett, Alex. "The Dilemma of Black Policemen." *Ebony* 7 (May 1971): 126-127.

"Prize Rookie." *Jet Magazine,* (June, 1955): 59.

Richardson, James F. *The New York Police.* New York: Oxford University Press, 1970.

Scott, Emmett. "Official History of the American Negro in World War." Federal Writers Project, 1919. Washington, D.C.: Howard University Library.

Snelson, Floyd. "Negro Policemen and Firemen." 27 July 1927 to 4 February 1930. Federal Writers Project (microfilm), Schomberg Collection, Reel 3, Article 28, n.p.

Spring 3100. "Police Facts." Bulletin No. 18, New York City Police Department, 1973.

Tenenbaum, Samuel. *Why Men Hate.* New York: Beechurst Press, 1947.

Thorpe, Earl E. *Black Historians.* New York: William Morrow and Co., Inc., 1971.

Tumin, Melvin M. *Social Stratification.* Englewood Cliffs, N.J.: Prentice-Hall, Inc., 1967.

U.S., Department of Commerce. Bureau of the Census. *United States Census of Population:* 1920. Vol. 1, *Characteristics of the Population,* New York.

————. Bureau of the Census. *Fifteenth Census of the United States Population,* 1930: Vol. 2.

————. Bureau of the Census. *United States Census of Population:* 1950, *Characteristics of the Population,* New York.

————. Bureau of the Census. *United States Census of Population:* 1960. Vol. 2, *Characteristics of Population* pt. 5, New York.

————. Bureau of the Census. *Statistical Abstract of the United States:* 1964, New York, (pp. 18, 19).

————. Bureau of the Census. *United States Census of Population:* 1970, *General Social and Economic Characteristics,* (pp. 402-26).

Weisman, Steven R. "How New York Became a Fiscal Junkie." *New York Times Magazine.* 17 August 1975, pp. 8, 9, 71-77.

Woodward, Vann C. *The Strange Career of Jim Crow.* Fairlawn, N.J.: Oxford University Press, 1966.

Work, Monroe N. "Chicago Leads all Other Cities in the Number of Negro Policemen." *Negro Yearbook.* Tuskegee, Ala.: Negro Yearbook Publishing Company, 1916-1917.

————. "Negro Policewomen." *Negro Yearbook.* Tuskegee, Ala.: Negro Yearbook Publishing Company, 1918-1919.

Wormser, Rene, *The Story of the Law.* New York: Simon & Schuster, 1962.

Young, Alfred J. Alfred J. Young Collection, New York City Police Department, Historian. New York.

# Index